PERFORMING RESEARCH
Tensions, triumphs and trade-offs of ethnodrama

PERFORMING RESEARCH
Tensions, triumphs and trade-offs of ethnodrama

Judith Ackroyd and
John O'Toole

A Trentham Book
Institute of Education Press, London

Institute of Education Press
20 Bedford Way
London
WC1H 0AL

First published 2010

British Library Cataloguing-in-Publication Data
A catalogue record for this book is available from the
British Library

ISBN 978 1 85856 446 3

Printed by CPI Group (UK) Ltd, Croydon, CR0 4YY

Contents

CONTENTS

Chapter 11
INVESTIGATING MASCULINITIES IN SCHOOL • 187
It's a play for us: ethnographic performance as part
of an educational ethnography

ACKNOWLEDGEMENTS

John and Judith would like to thank Griffith University Centre for Applied Theatre for the course and the colloquia, and Lil Hassall, Barbara Hogan and Roy Nevitt for their pioneering work. Also Neo Gwafila-Bulayani at Regent's College, London, for collating and formatting the text, and Puck Pilkington for her proof reading.

We also wish to acknowledge those academic/artist colleagues who have published in this area and those with whom we have discussed ideas. You know who you are. We toast Robby and Andy for their continued indulgence.

The authors of Chapter 6 say: 'We would like to express our appreciation of the support provided to us by Artistic and Creative Education at the University of Melbourne and to thank all of the women, present and past, whose stories have enriched our research, and our families, who seemed to understand our need to spend precious spare moments in our quest to create Alice'.

Jill Robinson wishes to thank the parents, children and the people working with them who participated in the evaluation of care co-ordination schemes, the project steering group and Julie Young for her excellent fieldwork.

The MA students in Hong Kong would like to thank the Faculty of Education, Griffith University, The Hong Kong Art School for the course and Penny Bundy for the teaching.

Linden Wilkinson wishes to thank Dr Michael Anderson and Dr John Hughes in The Faculty of Education and Social Work, The University of Sydney. Also, The National Institute of Dramatic Art (NIDA) Open Program for putting on the production of A Day in December and Jennifer Hagan for believing in the script and taking it to performance.

Richard Sallis wishes to express his thanks to the principal and teachers of Princes Hill Secondary College, Victoria, especially the drama department staff and to their drama classes who were such willing participants.

DEDICATION

To all the subjects of ethnodrama:
those communities, witnesses and respondents
– from students to scrap pickers and from accident
victims to nuns – who give parts of themselves up
for scrutiny by unknown audiences

Contributors

Jane Bird

Jane Bird is a Lecturer in Drama Education at The University of Melbourne. She has extensive experience in providing professional development and curriculum support for drama teachers. She has undertaken post-graduate research into the use of enactive and embodied drama processes to analyse and transform data into ethnographic performance.

Kate Donelan

Kate Donelan is Head of Drama Education at the University of Melbourne. Her ethnographic study of drama and intercultural learning in a secondary school won the 2007 American Alliance for Theatre and Education Distinguished Dissertation award. Her current ethnographic research investigates arts interventions with young people at risk.

Jumai Ewu

Jumai Ewu has served as workshop facilitator and resource person on Africa at international workshops and conferences. She researches and writes on Theatre for Development/Community Theatre, African Theatre and Performances. She is the editor of 'Theatre for Development: A Digest of Experiences', *Contemporary Theatre Review* Vol. 12 Parts 1 and 2, Routledge, 2002 and Associate Editor, *African Performance Review*, Adonis and Abbey. She is Senior Lecturer in Theatre and Performance in the School of the Arts, University of Northampton, UK.

Jill Robinson

Jill Robinson is currently Associate Dean for Teaching and Learning for the Faculty of Health at the University of East Anglia and is Co-Director for the Faculty's newly established Clinical Education Research Institute. She has a background in mental health nursing, social psychology and education and spent four years working in the Centre for Applied Research in Education at UEA as Course Director for their

Doctorate in Education. During that time she developed a growing interest in narrative research and the representation of experience. She has recently been pursuing this interest in the context of bringing research data into the classroom in ways that emotionally engage students in the experience of others.

Richard Sallis

Richard has written and given several ethnographic performances based on data collected in educational institutions. He lectures in drama/theatre education at the University of Melbourne where he is completing a PhD focusing on gender, educational ethnography and ethnographic performance. Richard is a former president of Drama Australia, the drama/theatre educators' association and is its current Director of International Liaison. He is a recipient of the Freda Cohen Award for the most meritorious Masters thesis (Research) in education.

Chris Sinclair

Chris Sinclair is a Senior Lecturer in Writing at Swinburne University and was most recently a Research Fellow in Arts Education at the University of Melbourne. She has taught acting, directing and performance making in universities. Her PhD examined rehearsal processes and aesthetic outcomes in community theatre practice.

Victor Ukaegbu

Victor I. Ukaegbu is Course Leader for Drama, University of Northampton. He is a performance practitioner and academic and has written widely on African and Intercultural theatres, Postcolonial performances, Gender, Black British theatre and Applied theatre. Recent publications include: 'The Gendered Misrepresentation of Women in Modern African Performance' in *African Performance Review*, 'The Problem with Definitions: An Examination of Applied Theatre in Traditional African Context(s)' in National Drama; 'Performing Postcolonially' in *World Literature Written in English (WLWE)* and two chapters in *Alternatives within the Mainstream*. He is an Associate Editor of *African Performance Review* and on the editorial boards of *World Scenography* (Africa/Middle East) and the *Journal of Applied Arts and Health*.

Prue Wales

Prue Wales is Assistant Professor in the Visual and Performing Arts Group at The National Institute of Education, Nanyang Technological University, Singapore. Her current research interests include narrative inquiry; ethnographic performance; and narrative identities expressed in stories using drama, digital media and multimodal forms.

Linden Wilkinson

Once very briefly an economist, Linden Wilkinson graduated from the National Institute of Dramatic Art (NIDA) with a Diploma in Acting in 1976. She worked extensively as a performer with major theatre companies in Sydney, Melbourne, Adelaide and Auckland and began writing plays in the mid 1980s. She has worked in television and documentaries as a writer, script editor and performer and continues to work in the theatre.

She returned to Sydney University in 2003. *Remembering Glenbrook* was the research for her Master's thesis. She continues to write and perform; she also teaches script writing in the NIDA Short Course program.

Estella Wong

Estella Wong is currently a full time lecturer in Drama and Theatre Education at the Hong Kong Academy for Performing Arts. She is involved in the teaching of the Master of Drama Education course co-presented by the Hong Kong Art School and Griffith University (Australia) as a part-time lecturer from 2004-08. Estella co-translated *Dramawise* (Brad Haseman and John O'Toole) into Chinese in 2005 and co-edited *Risks and Opportunities – the Tension in Hong Kong Drama Education Development* published by International Association of Theatre Critics Hong Kong (IATC) in 2007.

Preface

When people are discussing some particularly vivid real life experience, they commonly say 'You wouldn't read about it!' – with the unspoken sense that the experience itself and its live, shared retelling are both more credible than anything you might find in printed media. Yet that is just what research into social events and events is traditionally restricted to. Before it can be shared, the story of a community or other social phenomenon is reduced to words in print and passed through the fine and many-layered sieve of scholarly publication procedures. Whatever is left, apparently, is credible. This book is about the impetus among contemporary researchers to get back closer to the vivid and real-life experience 'that you wouldn't read about...'. Ethnographers and anthropologists, and also practitioners in fields such as health, education and human services whose effective practice is dependent on research in their contexts, are all looking for a way to re-create their discoveries and experiences for others, to replace the traditionally sanctioned way of chronicling research and its findings in written report or paper with some kind of live performance or re-presentation.

Originally brought together and possibly even first named 'ethnodrama' by anthropologists, at first sight this marriage of ethnography and drama seems a natural love match to both ethnographers and dramatic artists which is why there has been a generally uncritical early outpouring of enthusiasm. From the point of view of ethnographers, the idea of performing their reportage makes good sense. It's a natural development of the new-found confidence in celebrating rather than reducing the richness of rich data, and acknowledging the subjectivity of human research and the shifting and provisional nature of any knowledge about human society. Dramatic reconstruction provides a tempting model for re-creating the full three-dimensional richness of observed phenomena. From the point of view of a dramatic artist it also makes sense: after all playwrights research individuals and their communities to find the material for their plays. For playwrights specialising in documentary drama, community theatre, and using theatre as an educational vehicle, isn't it all part of the process? To re-create how a social context works, in order to give an audience new insights into that context?

This enthusiasm has led to a growing literature on the subject, in both books and journals, with projects chronicled in depth, and in some cases recorded as script or video/DVD. Most of this literature is overwhelmingly affirmative, mainly descriptions of projects that succeeded, at least for their authors. We are not alone in believing that the challenges in the form are at least as great as the achievements and that it is time for a balanced appraisal. This book sets out to stimulate and even create a critical dialogue about the live performance of research and research reportage that will both continue to map the territory and provide helpful signposts.

The soul of ethnodrama is face-to-face dialogue – turning the monologic statements of a written research report or a book like this into action, a contextualised performance which is viscerally received and can be interrupted ... many ethnodramas even make space for their audiences to interact in various ways. We can't reinvent the form of a book to make it a two-way conversation, dear readers, but the book is in itself already both dialogic and the product of dialogue. The numerous contributors to this book, including the authors, are all practitioners in the genre, who still regard ourselves as experimenters. The book started as many conversations, several practical and group-based university assignments and even a couple of formal colloquia between the authors and some of our contributors. Naturally some of our earliest dialogues took place with the growing literature, and also with the authors' own memories of ethnodramas which we had experienced as audience and as researcher-performers. We started to find that many of the artistic, social and scholastic tensions, as well as some assumptions and confusions common within the genre, are only partially acknowledged. We wanted to interrogate and illuminate them to aid both retrospective understanding and improved future practice. So we invited our brave discussants to create their own case studies, not just to chronicle their ethnodramatic achievements, but to scrutinise them together with us, within the critical frame of analysis provided by our exercise of mapping those tensions and assumptions.

What is in Section A

The first part of the book is comprised of this theoretical background and our own emerging critical framework. **Chapter 1** explores who does it, and why: the purposes for the researcher/performers themselves; for the target community and its respondents, participants or subjects; and for the audiences, including the almost improper-sounding question of how much fun it is. Our aim is to examine the whole movement; this includes the labels and definitions used. As we show in **Chapter 2**, there are quite a few labels, some of them warmly contested, even among ourselves. Our examination includes critically analysing the aims, diverse structures, and complex, often problematic outcomes of performed research. Any contract between human groups and the people researching them puts responsibilities on the latter. Two of these are explored in **Chapter 3**: the researcher's responsibility to society itself, including the contested question increasingly mooted in the literature that it is the place of ethnodrama not only to interpret and represent a community but to provide a broader platform for social action and social change; and the equally important and difficult ethical questions which surround any project that meddles in other people's business. **Chapter 4** continues exploring the responsibilities by mapping the inherent power relationships, in terms of questions of authority and authenticity; whose voices are represented, and how; and the relationships between the participants, the researchers and the many gatekeepers who may intervene. By definition, a merging of dramatic art and research methodology contains aesthetic tensions and entails artistic compromises, and imposes constraints on the form. This is truer still if there are other competing agendas to complicate the work further and provide new tensions – such as education or therapy. These tensions are explored in **Chapter 5**.

Though we take responsibility for the authorship of this section, there are three distinct sets of voice involved: besides our own voice, we have tried to represent the key voices from the literature, and also what our contributors have to say on the subject. To assist this distinction, we have adopted the convention of quoting directly from the literature, but paraphrasing our contributors' ideas and opinions. (We have member-checked them to make sure we're not misrepresenting them!). Some of these paraphrased statements and assertions do not exist in the final case studies of the contributors to whom they are attributed; those we took from earlier drafts, or from their conversations with the authors. This is part of the dialogue.

What is in Section B

The contributors' case studies provide the second part of the book and we hope they both illuminate Section A, and create a new conversation. Like everything else in this field, there are many disparities and un-answered questions, both among the case studies, and also challenging our own tentative conclusions in Section A. In the six chapters there are ten examples of ethnodrama which span three cultural *milieus*: Australia, England and Hong Kong. Some of their authors are experienced researchers, some experienced performers and some relative beginners in both fields, though all bring some area of relevant expertise, a sharp and questioning intelligence, and a willingness to investigate their own work critically.

We asked a lot from our case study contributors, much more than we gave them in return. We asked them to

> tell the story of the project, as comprehensively as is possible within the word limits, and also critically, raising and discussing the themes, issues and ques-tions that arose during or as a result of the project. By 'critically' we mean that you should try to reveal and acknowledge as fairly as is possible the range of successes, triumphs, negotiations, tensions, trade-offs, difficulties, dis-appointments and unfinished business. This discussion should be related to the themes, issues and questions raised in Section A.

We asked them in their accounts to provide the outline of the whole project, its motivation and origins, personal and professional; their pre-ferred terminology, and why; the researchers' own positioning, their influences and their own stake in the research; which community was involved as participants, subjects or witnesses; which audiences they had or envisaged; who were the other stakeholders, and why. We also asked for a brief outline or summary of the performance piece, including snippets of script and, where appropriate, a sample of voices from the witnesses and community, the researchers and the audience(s).

And that was just the start. What we were even more interested in was the themes, issues, and negotiations they pursued; their key decisions, any changes of direction and the reasons for them; the problems and tensions that arose, particularly between research, aesthetic form and other purposes; what learnings emerged from the project as a whole, and from the process as distinct from the performance; and any other special features of the project.

We also asked them: 'What are its research influences, and how is your particular research paradigm or methodology underpinned or manifested in the project?' In retrospect, this request was unnecessary, since that was bound to come out as they addressed the copious requirements above and it did. However, some of them responded to this in spades, giving us the full benefit of their impressive scholarship, to the extent that it threatened to turn the book into a multi-volume research encyclopaedia. Regretfully, we pillaged this generous offering to embed within Section A – with which most of their perspectives tallied closely – and enrich its theoretical substance, and then asked them to remove virtually all of it from their own chapters. You might find some of it published elsewhere, and if so, we recommend you read it!

Though we started with the notion of two-way and regular dialogue, where 'we will be happy to discuss your queries and ideas with you, and in turn we will keep you in touch with our progress and ideas', we then closed down one useful opening for them: 'In order for the case studies to retain their individual integrity, we would be grateful if you do not discuss your chapter with other case study authors'!

As if that wasn't enough, we asked too if they had any tips to pass on to other potential ethnographic performer/researchers. We had intended to finish the book with a brief set of 'guidelines' for intending ethno-dramatists. We wanted to provide a tentative little SWOT guide to find the Strengths and Opportunities, and avoid the Weaknesses and Threats, which we hope we have identified in these pages. After writing the chapters which follow, we realised that this would have been both impertinent and rash.

How to read this book

You can read our chapters first, or begin with a case study, depending on your experience of the genre. If you aren't very familiar, you may be advised to begin with a couple of case studies, so you get a sense of the sort of work that might be included in the term ethnodrama, or whichever of the alternative nomenclature identified in Chapter 2 you prefer. If you are one of those would-be ethnodramatic adventurers, we suggest that you trawl the book for useful hints from the experiences of the case studies, or our own commentaries and analysis... but, like any buyer, *caveat emptor*, and good luck.

1

THE HUMAN CONTEXTS

Who performs research, and why

> There was a story to be told that wasn't adequately represented by our report, not because the report didn't say these things but because it didn't quite reflect the humanity of what was provided nor the personal experience of the everyday lives of the parents who took part. (Jill, Chapter 7)

First, it was anthropologists who started exploring the notion of performing research, with ethnographers hot on their heels. Performing research makes a great deal of sense to both anthropologists and ethnographers – at first sight, anyway. If you are an anthropologist, your job is to study and record the human species in the wild: ie its behaviour individually and socially. If you are an ethnographer your job is to study and record the social behaviour of humans in groups and communities. 'Study and record' sounds simple, but the phrase conceals another word: 'transform', which must be faced at the outset, as it starts happening from the very first choices we make about how we will study, let alone record, our quarry.

Fortunately, most anthropologists and ethnographers long ago realised two important differences between themselves and other biologists: the complexity and constantly dynamic nature of human society means that there are only so many things you can usefully measure and quantify, and also that you can't get more than a superficial impression by studying the phenomenon from the outside. So the scientific ideal and mythical position of being the dispassionate and neutral outsider, like a botanist coming to understand the specimen through observation and recording it in a natural or naturalistic setting, was not really an option. Botanists have little choice to do much else, other than destroy it by cutting it up. However, some zoologists, like some ethnographers, have found that with some animals the best way to understand their behaviour is to get up close and dirty, to engage with the fauna and, most importantly, as much as possible on its own terms. Think of Jane Goodall mixing it with her demonic chimps and peaceful bonobos (1986), or Konrad Lorenz nearly fifty years ago (1964) with a menagerie from ducks to wolves.

This has also exonerated the human behavioural observers from pretending to be exact sciences and for many has replaced the very word 'scientist' with 'investigator' or 'researcher'. It has also brought serious responsibilities. One of these is to try and understand with some accuracy and insight, and insight does mean getting *inside* the community. Otherwise, the reporters can too easily find themselves in the position of the sort of sad anthropologist evoked by Kieran Egan, who gathered from their research that the LoDagaa, an illiterate indigenous people, could not count. When LoDagaa were asked to count they looked blank and said 'Count...? What?' so the scientist assumed they were expressing ignorance of the notion of counting. Eventually, it turned out that in fact they had several distinct and sophisticated systems of counting, unlike their primitive Western guest, and their question was a genuine attempt to help this dumb stranger to specify what it was they were required to count (Egan, 1988:103).

In other words, the observable and experience-able behaviour of the community all passes through the mincer of the researcher's purposes (what they are trying to find out, and why), interpretation (of what the behaviour means), selection (of what is deemed to be important) and transformation (into something the researcher can find meaningful). This includes recognising similarities and disparities within the researcher's own experience as a member of another human community – or multiple communities.

And that's just the first stage, because the mince is going to emerge somehow at the other end of the mincing machine, to be devoured or consumed like any mince – since the purposes of researchers include disseminating the results to someone. Nobody does research to then hide what they've found. We return to the question of purposes later in this chapter, after looking briefly at who is going to consume it, and how it's going to be cooked. To continue the metaphor, the standard cooking method of a written report, another hangover of the scientific tradition, is the equivalent of boiling the mince until most of the taste and nutrition has evaporated, and serving it completely ungarnished, palatability not being a necessary concomitant of truth in the scientific tradition.

At first sight a marriage of ethnography and drama seems to ethnographers and dramatic artists to be a natural love match, which is why there has been a generally uncritical early outpouring of enthusiasm. From the point of view of ethnographers, the idea of performing their reportage makes good sense. It's a natural development of the new-found confidence in acknowledging the subjectivity of their human research and of celebrating rather than reducing the richness of rich data. Dramatic reconstruction provides a tempting model for re-creating the full three-dimensional richness of observed phenomena.

Obviously working ethnographers make mincemeat of data all the time, by drawing conclusions, making selections and drawing parallels. These transformations may be said to be enriching, since their aim is to create new meanings for the research subjects or the 'others' of potential audiences. Inevitably however, the documentation and representation process entails a number of layers of progressive impoverishment. Consider a common and simple ethnographic technique. Suppose you are the ethnographer, conducting an interview with two willing informants. As the researcher, you've done your backgrounding well enough, and have engaged with or lived with the subjects. Consequently you are in a position to know how they might be likely to react so devise questions that are appropriate and ask them in ways that are sensitive to the subjectivities of both the subjects and yourself. Already there is a complex network of history and your relationship with the interviewees, which are all an important part of how the interview will happen. In the interview:

■ As it happens in real life and three dimensions, you can see the informants' movements, their paralanguage, the chemistry be-

3

tween them, hear the exact tones and timing of their utterances, probably both touch and smell them, and move yourself into whatever proxemic relationship you think will help.

■ Video it, and you've lost one complete dimension, though you can still hear and partially see them.

■ Audiotape it, and you've lost another.

■ Write down their comments, or transcribe them from the tapes, and you've lost all direct contact with the informants and the living nature of their data – at best you can reproduce it through verbal description: eg *Pause, five seconds. Informant A scratches head; Informant B shrugs.*

■ Get somebody else to transcribe it, and there is not even a memory of the visceral and the emotional content, nor of the relationships expressed in the dialogue.

Months or years later, enshrined in the pages of a book or journal, this impoverishment ironically takes on the unjustifiable mantle of truthfulness. For one thing it's in print, which means it has been acknowledged by peers to be true. For another, print is unchanging so what we read today about that encounter will be just as true tomorrow, even though the interview represents only a moment in the informants' lives, possibly an untypical and certainly simplified moment and their own truths will have moved on.

Re-creating a research site through performance makes particularly good sense from a post-structuralist perspective. The phenomena of human behaviour are so complex, so dynamic, so protean and so negotiable, involving the ongoing lives of the subjects and the shifting and variable meanings made out of these by the observers. So a form of reportage that maintains all the dimensions of the original interaction or observation can perhaps provide a valuable holding form. More than that, one of the characteristics of drama is that participants – actors and audience – put themselves into others' shoes, empathising with the subjects of the drama while simultaneously maintaining distance and detachment through the celebrated 'dual affect'. This may make the research site and the subjects' lives accessible subjectively, emotionally and existentially for the researcher and reader to identify with 'this other'.

A further potential enrichment is that drama works through creating metaphors, embodied analogies which seem to have a life of their own and can provide new perspectives on the familiar or the lived. By re-creating the research site in metaphorical terms such as dramatic fiction or symbolic movement, the researchers may be able to expose some of the unspoken or unrecognised sub-texts of the subject community. Can they create new insights for the researchers and subjects alike?

From the point of view of a dramatic artist, this kind of re-creation of researched communities appears to make sense: after all, playwrights research individuals and their communities to come up with the material for their plays. For the playwrights specialising in documentary drama, community theatre, and using theatre as an educational vehicle, isn't it all part of the process? We re-create how a social context works to give an audience new insights into that context. If our aim is community expression, where the audience is the community itself, can we use the re-creation to help the community to find a voice and express or celebrate its identity, or even achieve a therapeutic purpose?

By this point, in this golden vista of a new research age, alarm bells should be ringing. The problem comes down to the relationships and implications between differences of purpose that are usually unacknowledged. The main purpose of this book is to identify and map these relationships and implications, to uncover the tensions and to see whether and how they are being addressed and whether and how the manifestations of ethnographic performance can be effective as research, representation of community, art or something else entirely, or even a blend of these.

Purposes

Starting with the researchers, initially it seems that the number of purposes are limited. There are as yet only a few research contexts which employ ethnodrama practices with any frequency: predominantly education, sociology and social anthropology, and occasionally business and commerce. All these industries need to explore and understand how communities work: A large number of ethnodramas are generated in research training – not least in drama and theatre studies departments of universities which see as irresistible the opportunity to kill two birds with one stone, by developing community drama skills and research skills at the same time. To the above list of research contexts should be added a major 'new' player: health and social medicine, whose practitioners are drawn towards both the communicative and the empathic properties of drama, in the search for personal and social well-being, and even therapy.

Jill's words, which head this chapter, are significant. Her re-creation of a community was not the work of a cool and disinterested research investigator, but a healthcare professional and health educator whose report was intended as a document that would have an impact on her own working context and an outcome beyond itself. She wanted to try and use a dramatic form to bring her research findings into the classroom in the form of a script to use with health professional students. Her work introduced another motivation for the research, and a new dynamic beyond reportage or representation. Her main purpose was shaped by her audience, who were students whose purpose was to learn about the details of healthcare which Jill was trying to teach them. As she reveals, she had a broader audience purpose too. She felt there was a story to be told that wasn't adequately represented by her team's research report about the parents of chronically ill children. That was not because the report didn't say the relevant things but that it didn't quite reflect the humanity of what was provided nor the personal experience of the everyday lives of the parents who took part.

As her chapter explains, both the research method and the form of the dramatised report are significantly mediated by her purposes towards her informants and the choices she made relating to their purposes and needs in the encounters which formed her ethnographic performance: 'In the end I didn't use the extract. The risk of revealing the parent's identity was too great'. Jill also had another audience, whose needs and sensitivities were considerably more demanding and more critical than her students'. This was the community of parents from which participants had been recruited. To illustrate what she had done, she sent them a copy of the script, filmed a reading of it, and made a DVD. The parents she met disseminated the script to their full membership and invited comments.

Early ethnographic performances tended to operate from the assumption that the single audience would comprise the researcher's peers, who would be 'reading' the performance from a standpoint of detached interest, as in a standard scientific research report or article. Almost invariably, and certainly in nearly all the most well-known or documented examples of the genre, this is not the case. At the simplest level, the informants, or members of the informants' community, are often either present in the audience, or form a separate audience for the presentation. For example, the researcher-performers of an ethnodrama seeking to capture something of the essence of a Norwegian football supporters' club gave two performances: the first in their university, to their research colleagues, and the second, in the supporters' club itself. The two performances were received very differently, as we shall see.

Beyond these two clearly and simply definable audiences drawn from the research community and the informants' community, we can see how the purposes widen as the audience widens. In the often documented ethnodramas of Jim Mienczakowski, he makes it clear that other researchers are not the only, nor even the primary, audience and nor are the informants. However, not least because they were forming at least part of the audience for the ethnodramas, he felt a strong sense of responsibility to honour his informants' statements:

> The script is guided by informants and plurally voices their agenda ... and insights and explanations gleaned from the performances are consensually negotiated ... such elements of negotiation are particularly important in the validatory phase of such projects when audiences are entirely drawn from the research environment hosting the project. (1998)

His informants and primary audience in the ethnodramas he was writing about here actually comprise two largely but not entirely separate audiences: healthcare consumers, and healthcare professionals. He had a major and quite different purpose other than reporting research: to use it in a reflexive therapeutic capacity with those informants, a purpose which he acknowledges as controversial: 'Since 1992 the therapeutic potential of ethnodramas for health consumers has been the subject of much debate' (*ibid*:26).

The ethnodramas referred to here were all commissioned by a range of healthcare agencies, who formed a third audience. In any case he had intentions towards yet another audience which was different again by being external: not the interested gaze of health consumers, nor even the more disinterested gaze of fellow researchers but the complex and diverse responses of students attending a theatre-in-education performance: 'The same issues have further been used by school and university arts and education students as the basis for discussion and work on the social construction of illness' (*ibid*:26). And he foresees a broader audience yet, and another dimension of purpose: 'Ethnodramas must seek audiences from beyond the world of health, in order to widen general understanding' (*ibid*:80). These diverse functional agendas, particularly the therapeutic intent, raise and leave unanswered the question of whether Mienczakowski's work is in fact ethnography in the true sense of the term.

The other case studies in this book reveal equally complex webs of motivation and purpose for the researchers, and needs, demands or expectations from the audiences. The Hong Kong students' primary purpose was quite simple and clear; creating group ethnodramas was the basis of an assignment which they had to pass in order to gain their Master's degree. Their assignment was designed much in the spirit of this book and by one of the co-authors. As they created and performed their ethnodramas, their task was to be documenting and analysing the dynamics of the process and the relationships, synergies and tensions between their various roles as researchers, playwrights and actors, chroniclers of various community behaviours and members of the audiences of each others' works. Not surprisingly they were all nervous before the single performance: their results depended on it, their apprentice artistry as playwrights and actors was under professional scrutiny and their peers were also watching and evaluating. However, they were sustained by their commitment to their research topics and the informants they had found – in particular the Scrap Pickers group was very buoyed by the discoveries they had made about their subjects, and the unexpected respect they had found for them, and wanted to share this with the audience, and convey to it how their own initially patronising approaches had been subverted. As Will from that group noted, before their project went out to educate their intended audience, they had educated themselves first.

Linden's study is partially driven by the same motivation, creating and documenting her ethnodrama formed her thesis for a Master's degree. The subject itself (a fatal train crash and its effects on survivors) was suggested by a chance personal encounter, which resonated with her own situated experience and sense of the local community in which she lived, and raised a key question she wanted to investigate. As a playwright and active theatrical professional she was also interested in the form of verbatim theatre, which she perceived as dovetailing with her ethnographic study of her subject.

Richard too is a student, creating an ethnodrama as his field study towards completing his doctoral degree. Unlike the other students, he is an independent research student, who could have chosen any topic for his research and any form of research report. He chose ethnodrama partly in order to study the dynamics of ethnodramas. This PhD study is the second significant study he has devoted both to ethnodrama (his master's degree report included an ethnodrama script too) and to the same subject area, exploring how students construct and understand masculinities in school settings. However, as well as significant shifts in his school settings and informants' groups, his *modus operandi* and his intended audiences, he has shifted the emphasis of study much more towards the nature, dynamics and structure of ethnodrama, which forms one of his two research questions. In his earlier study ethnodrama was merely the form which he chose to evoke and report his findings on masculinities in a school. One of his underlying aims was to ascertain the usefulness of an ethnographic performance written as part of an educational ethnography from the perspective of those within the research setting and the ethnographer. This time he has quite an audience web: both primary sets of student informants and various other key informants at different status levels, such as teachers and school administrators, the peers of those two primary sets of informants who form a public audience ... and of course his examiners, and not forgetting those research peers who will read his findings in research journals ... such as the readers of this book. And to further complicate his network of purpose and audience, since he is contributing to this book prior to completion of his PhD, his contribution is presumably having some effect on the study itself.

Victor and Jumai had no such self-sufficient research study aim. As they trenchantly indicate, the triple aims of their research performance were to provide an alternative platform for the teaching of Black British history in schools, an entertaining framework for enhancing the public understanding of black presence in Northamptonshire in general and a critical exploration of the different experiences of immigration. Examining these in reverse, the last is most in tune with the notion of pure and disinterested research, at least at face value. A 'critical exploration of different experiences' is appropriate for a classic ethnography. However this bland statement on its own would effectively mask their positioning and ideological intentions, which were a deeper set of purposes than that of adding to the sum of human knowledge. Victor and Jumai themselves have experiences and access to other family experiences of immigration,and a passionate personal interest (in both senses of that word) in the experiences of immigrants. The second of the aims reveals another double purpose: both to entertain, and to 'enhance public understanding' or to educate the audiences by changing their understanding or giving them some new understanding about the local presence of black people. We note that this sentence is the first time the word 'entertain' has been mentioned in this chapter, which for most of the population is the primary purpose, if not the only one, for a dramatic performance of any kind. Victor and Jumai's first aim goes further still in ambition, well beyond the audiences who actually come to see the performed research, to a notional audience of the most influential teachers and policymakers of history in schools. It boldly asserts its intention to change the whole practice of teaching history by providing 'an alternative platform'.

Of the case studies we have chosen, the one which comes closest to being a piece of performed research which resulted from a 'pure' attempt to discover and present knowledge for its own sake to an audience of peers is the ethnographic performance created in several iterations by the team of women: Kate, Jane, Prue and Chris, whom we collectively call 'Alice' after their eponymous hero. The single-mindedness of their purpose and their restricted audiences suggests that their work might be simpler to analyse than that of the others, whose purposes and audiences were complex and compromised. The simplicity is apparent rather than real. Alice phrase their aim clearly and articulately. As researchers they endeavoured to report on the nature of ethnographic performance, displaying its ephemeral and reflexive properties. They hoped the participants-as-audience would respond to the performance in an almost Brechtian way, as thoughtful observers, before engaging in the themes of the work as collaborators and active and engaged performance makers in the ensuing workshop.

In a sense their work is almost meta-research and meta-performance (researching research and performing performance) since, like Richard, they were interested in the nature and form of ethnographic performance itself, as they themselves created and structured it, and as it was received by its audiences. They also refer to the 'themes of our work', however, which gives away that the performance, while it may have a reflexive dimension, is more than just self-reflexive. Alice comes close to 'auto-ethnography' in that though there are a range of informants, in the end the major informants are themselves, and they are dramatising many of their own experiences. But not just any experiences, in order to stake their identity or parade their self-presentation on the stage. Their specific focus is on women academics in an Australian university, with particular reference to one university, from which the audience can generalise if they wish. Behind that, for all of them as a group and individuals, there is an ideological drive, just as deep as for Victor and Jumai, which is about revealing the experiences of women in university life, and of women in relation to the power structures and the logistics of power in academia throughout the twentieth century, as well as through their own contemporary experience. While the three main performances of the piece have all been to a fairly closed audience of academic peers, each of those audiences has had slight but important differences.

The first audience, at a faculty colloquium, was comprised of close colleagues and friends of Alice, all familiar with the University and the contextual reference points, experienced in research and conventional research reports but not all drama-savvy. Some were disposed to be academically critical, which was their job at the colloquium. The second audience was at an international drama conference, where all the audience was drama-savvy and again disposed to be critical but few were experienced in research; about half knew or knew of the performer/researchers, and almost none knew the contextual reference points. The third audience was at an international research conference, where performed ethnography was one of the themes; all the audience were experienced researchers, but few were drama-skilled; few knew the performers, or the specific university reference points, although many came from similar university contexts.

Alice anticipated and took these differences into account in preparing each version of the performance and accompanying workshop, which was part of the performance event for the audience. Like the Hong Kong students they shared considerable anxiety before their performances but for a quite different reason. Not only were they under scrutiny as artists and performers, about which their second audience in particular would be knowledgeably critical, they were also putting up aspects of their own lives and identities for scrutiny about how they were choosing to reconstruct themselves.

Respondents and witnesses

The researchers all share one thing in common, which is also shared by the great majority of ethnographic performance researchers: they all chose the community they were going to research. For example, Richard is interested in masculinities and had access to a school with appropriate student groups; the Hong Kong Scrap Pickers team chose that community as one they were interested in discovering more about and set about finding it. Some, a much smaller number, are created in response to a request from an outside agency, like some of Mienczakowski's, such as a youth drugs and alcohol or mental health agency.

In a sense, Victor and Jumai's performance was in response to the researchers' hunch that the community of black immigrants in Northampton might appreciate their story being told. However, none of the examples in this chapter, or anywhere else that we have found, have been at the explicit request of the community being researched, except where that community is the researchers researching themselves: the auto-ethnographers mentioned in chapter two and, up to a point, Alice. In cases like Victor and Jumai's the reason they proposed the project themselves might be just because the members of that community had no concept of a research-based performance of their lives and experience which they could articulate into a request; otherwise they probably would have. In a few cases the decision seems to have been made jointly by the researchers and the researched, such as Johnny Saldaña's *Maybe someday, if I'm famous* performance, itself now famous, which is explored later. This was a joint performance of the life and experiences of a young actor, by the researcher and an actor, which the research subject was willing and enthusiastic to have retold as performance – well, most of it (Saldaña, 1998).

For a significant number of the researched, the appellation 'subject' is more appropriate than 'participant', since initially the researchers' approach to them was unsolicited, and came at the instigation either of the researchers, or the agency for which they were working. For a few, the idea that they would instigate a performance about their own experiences is almost unthinkable: for the community of Laramie, for instance, who became the subjects of one of the most famous of ethnodramas, *The Laramie Project*, dealing with a homophobic killing in the town (Kaufman, 2001). Linden's witnesses are similar: they were in any case an accidental and very unwilling community, linked only by their experiences as participants in a train crash. For these communities, spectacularly, and for many other individuals and communities who have found themselves the subjects of ethnographic performance, a crucial key to the viability of the project was the sensitivity of the approach. This would have needed to include a clear explanation by the researchers of their intentions, their own purposes in wanting to create such an event. The Laramie Project team cleverly and honestly reveal as part of their performance itself how the community was mixed in its response, and some of the reasons which underlay the refusals, partial consents and withdrawals that the team faced.

This indicates that there are many potential tensions between the purposes of the researchers and those of the researched, which are not always explicitly acknowledged or effectively dealt with in the performances. Researchers invariably make every effort to scrupulously record the experiences of their witnesses, and honour them by re-telling them (re-depicting them) truthfully, or at least they intend to. But what do those words 'honour' and 'truth' mean, and what effect does the interpretation have on the re-telling? And where there are tensions with other interested parties, or with other dimensions of the whole production, such as conflicts between the audience's needs and the witnesses' goodwill. Who wins and who loses? These questions will be dealt with in more detail in Chapters 3 and 4.

The points of view and requirements of the audience

In terms of the researchers' purposes, the audience and its needs sometimes figure crucially, sometimes barely at all. The researchers select their audiences based on a wide range of expectations and preconceptions as to what those audiences will get out of the performance and how they will react. Of all the writers of our case studies, Alice probably corresponds most closely to the early notional audience – a closed and homogeneous group of 'research peers', at least for the first and last of their performances. Even here, as we have seen, there were distinctions between the audiences for the three performances; Alice identified those audience distinctions precisely and revised or fine-tuned the script and the actual performance presentations specifically to address them.

The subjects or community participants of ethnodrama themselves are at least one of the audiences for almost all ethnographic performances and invariably have a big stake in what they see and hear. Obviously, in the case of Jill's respondents, it was necessary for her to exercise extreme sensitivity and not take any liberties at all with what they or others might misconstrue. Besides not risking using one vivid contribution in case the anonymity was compromised, Jill also notes that the meaning of the extract in isolation from the individual character of the parent would probably not have been characteristic.

This audience of respondents demands that the performance should be in some way representative or 'authentic'. This may need more insight than the researchers are able to achieve. The ethnodrama setting out to depict something of the nature and dynamics of a Norwegian football supporters' club started off with two serious handicaps: the research team had limited time to research and create the performance, and they wittingly gave themselves the enormous extra hurdle that all four of them were young women who did not like football, and were not sympathetic to the very concept of a footy fan club. In fact, their own purposes (one of which was that this was an assignment for a master's course) also included the unusual and brave one of deliberately choosing this context in order to discover something new about a subject they really did not understand at all, and have their preconceptions challenged. Bully for them, but it meant they took quite a significant proportion of their time finding out sufficient rudiments of the club, the game and the culture of football and football supporters to be able to connect with their respondents. Then they had to make more than rudimentary sense of what the respondents were talking about, before they could start tuning into the dynamics and shared meanings of their witnesses. They boldly performed their ethnodrama at the supporters' club to an audience including both the original witnesses and their kindred. The researchers' interviews with members of this audience indicate that they enjoyed the show; they appreciated the event either as an honour that they were the focus of research or as a joke, or both. They applauded the girls for their audacity and their theatrical skills, but they were politely guarded about the show's authenticity, and about whether it had much to say about them or their lifestyle or their football club.

But how much fun is it?

To go back to the origins of research, fun doesn't figure in either of the great historical traditions: the academic tradition of Logos, which means seeking truth through the exploration of what is already known and passed down – ie the grand literature review, or the scientific tradition of Logic, which means seeking it through observation, experimentation and data gathering and the ruthless paring down of possibilities to what is left. Whether you are seeking eternal truths or a cure for cancer, when you pick up a research journal or book, you are not looking for an entertaining read. On the contrary, if you find one, it means that there's something interfering between you and the reception and assumption of what can be trusted, which at the very least is an emotional response or a creative, and thus unreliable, dissonance.

Where does that put ethnodrama practitioners and their audiences? This is where two of the distinct meanings of the word 'interest' become important – ie 'holding attention' and 'having a stake in' (the antonyms 'uninterested' and 'disinterested' express the distinction clearly). The first thing to note is that the audiences are not the usual research audience: the only people who pick up a scientific or academic research journal are other researchers in the same or an allied field, who have a specific interest (in the sense of having a stake and thus a need to know). This kind of research peer audience is a small fraction of the audience for ethnodrama. Even for the first and last audiences of *Alice Hoy is not a building*, or the audience of Saldaña's *Barry's Story*, the word 'drama' does change the expectation. The university colloquium watching *Alice's* debut did not expect a solemn disquisition: they came along in a lively, sympathetic and talkative manner, quite a few brought friends, relatives or other colleagues, and the atmosphere before the beginning, which was accompanied with wine and refreshments, resembled the cheerful anticipation in a theatre foyer much more than a typical research lecture. They were mostly disinterested but not uninterested, expecting to be informed *and* entertained, to have their attention engaged and held. Their response indicated that this was so, and some of them also indicated that they valued and took on board the latter more than the former. Part of the entertainment and their engagement was provided by the information and another part was the resistance for some audience members to some of what they were seeing; they wanted to take issue or interrogate the data being presented. The ensuing discussion and workshop gave the whole event a dynamic which certainly contributed to the meanings which were constructed for audience and research/performers alike and taken away by both. The dialogue was part of the performance, in a broad sense, and therefore part of the research. Alice recognised this, dutifully recorded it and incorporated some of the new meanings in their next iteration. Much the same was no doubt present for Victor and Jumai's performance.

Some ethnographic performers, especially students, go out hunting for a community which is likely to have some built-in potential for entertainment, both in the data gathering for themselves, and in the performance. Both these were in the minds of Barb and Lil, two Master's students embarking on a student ethnodrama, when they chose the topic and the rather curious community of internet sex and intimacy consumers. This choice was partly to satisfy their own curiosity and partly to entertain themselves with the double challenge of entering and documenting this community and of finding effective and appropriate theatrical form for communicating it to their own assessors and research peers, though not to the invisible community of their subjects.

They succeeded in transforming their own engagement sufficiently well into effective theatre that the piece was reprised to mixed approbation and considerable admiration at a national drama conference. The respondent community's verdict on its success as accurate and respectful ethnography is not known.

Richard and the Hong Kong teams were all more circumspect in their choices of community to research. Their quest was similar: although in all cases their audiences were connected to the research, the concept of entertainment and engagement were built in. They are drama students, after all, and aesthetic pleasure was one of the dimensions all were exploring. Any of the teams of Hong Kong drama students would have been embarrassed to bore their audience of fellow researcher/ performers with a performance that was worthy but dull, which is not a consideration for many academic research presenters in other fields. Richard's audiences were different, namely the respondents themselves, in other words the youngsters who had provided the data from which the performance was constructed. Although they were students and therefore a captive audience, he had a duty to ensure they had an enjoyable and satisfying time; some of this would be provided, as he indicates, by their pleasure at seeing themselves represented and/or transformed. This was the duty of the Norwegian 'football team'. Their audience of respondents, the football supporters in their clubroom, certainly weren't going to bother to stick around for something they found boring, and some would certainly have come with baggage of preconceptions about 'research' and 'academics'. The team won the 'engagement' match: they kept their audience in the room and relatively happy. As accurate ethnography the respondents rated it no better than a draw; in soccer parlance, the defence was full of holes.

For any ethnographic performers, where the audience is broader still, entertainment becomes a real issue. Tara Goldstein and Jim Mienczakowski are both ethnodramatists who use the work they create for explicitly educational purposes: as Mienczakowski says 'to widen general understanding'. The inevitable tensions which this creates between aesthetic, educational and research purposes and dynamics will be mapped in detail in Chapters 3 and 4, but part of the tension is that entertaining and engaging the audience is a factor which needs to be taken into account, though neither Goldstein nor Mienczakowski really addresses this question. For Goldstein, at least, engaging the audience or at least not putting them off is an important part of the equation, but that's as far as she gets: 'I ... wanted my ethnographic findings and analyses to speak to schoolteachers and administrators rather than at them' (2002:2). Mienczakowski's accounts (eg 1994, 1997) are squarely about planning for the researcher/performers' purposes, not the audience's – in Geoff Gillham's classic phrase: 'the play for the teachers, not the play for the children' (1974). In discussion with this author, Mienczakowski has on more than one occasion indicated that his priorities lie elsewhere, in his responsibilities to honour his respondents' offerings, and to transform them as little as possible for any purpose of either entertainment or aesthetic values.

Such a firm stance is not a luxury available to those who make their living by theatre, however socially conscious, and where general audiences are concerned the word ethnodrama is entirely absent. However, the genre is around, in numerous manifestations in fringe and community theatre, One practitioner has an extraordinary capacity to understand the entertainment dimension. Though he doesn't call himself a performance ethnographer, we would certainly classify Moises Kaufman as one, and at least two of the works with which he has been involved – Tectonic Theatre's *The Laramie Project* (Kaufman, 2001) and the indirectly auto-ethnographical *I am my own wife* (Wright, 2004) have both hit the big-time global theatre scene, including both Broadway and international productions. And that kind of exposure brings its own responsibilities. Well, all public performance is exposure, which brings responsibilities to those who lie behind its creation; Broadway's is just bigger than most. To investigate the responsibilities of exposing yourself or others is where we head in Chapter 3, after providing more exact definition of the phenomenon we are studying.

2
CHARTING THE TERRITORY

Ethnodrama and its close relations

The authors of the case studies described in Section B refer to their work in different ways yet all appear in a book on ethnodrama. Alice refer to their project as 'an ethnographic performance', Jill writes of her 'Reader's Theatre' and Linden describes her 'Verbatim Theatre play'. Richard talks of his role as an educational ethnographer and is happy to use the terms ethnodrama and ethnographic performance interchangeably. Victor and Jumai refer to community theatre. Only our Hong Kong MA students commit to the term ethnodrama and this may be because they are studying a course with ethnodrama in the title! Clearly, we, the authors, have made decisions about what we understand to constitute ethnodrama or ethnodramatic practices, and chose the case studies accordingly. But are the various terms synonymous or are there distinctions? What is the relationship between practices described as ethnodrama, ethnographic performance, documentary theatre and verbatim theatre? And how do these connect with a notion of performing research? This chapter considers the landscape of these practices, exploring what determines the use of different labels.

The transience of labels

Let us go back to the 1980s. A new town, Milton Keynes, was created in the heart of England. The Living Archive Project, developed as a challenge to the popular view that a new town has no history, attracted national and international acclaim. An early example of the Project emerged through the vivid and extraordinary stories of a survivor of the first world war, Hawtin Mundy. His stories were recorded, enabling Roy Nevitt and his collaborators to tell them through performance. The Project was committed to exploring the 'rich resource on everyone's doorstep' believing the 'history of the places where we live lies dormant in documents and in people's memories.' (www.livingarchive.org.uk). A home front second world war piece, for instance, used local council documents. These revealed that some people didn't wish to take in evacuees and described the tricks they used to avoid doing so. A newly wedded wife was found to have been fined for putting stale bread in the rubbish bin instead of the bin for pigswill. It emerged that she was trying to be thrifty and use rationed food as wisely as she could. She was ashamed that she had saved the bread too long, and feared that if she put it in the pig swill, she might be found out for being so wasteful in times of need.

So what were Nevitt and his colleagues doing? Nevitt called it documentary theatre. He never described the work as research or research in performance, nor as performance ethnography nor ethnodrama. Since his work engaged members of the community in the performances, he also talked of community theatre. But how might we describe the work of Nevitt and The Living Archive Project today? Once upon a time, those of us who reflected on our lessons and roles as classroom teachers were just instinctively doing what we thought would help us do our jobs better. Now we would identify ourselves as reflective practitioners and this makes us teachers who are involved in research activity. Now we understand the context of our enquiry within a research paradigm, but we have a different notion of research and its relationship with practice.

Roy Nevitt gathered data from people in the community in which he lived. Often it was historical data and it always involved interviews with people to gather their stories on tape. This may be conceived as historical research. It is what Linden does in her preparation for the performance about a train accident. It is what the historians did who prepared the data for the Northamptonshire Black History Group that led to Victor and Jumai's project. It is what the Hong Kong groups carried out with their various participant groups.

Nevitt engaged those who had given their narratives in the development of the work. Hawtin Mundy was fully involved in the transformation of his words into performance. A variety of theatrical conventions was employed, often including song and sometimes dance. This work fulfils one of Jones's three key principles for ethnographic performance: that it should grow as a collaboration between ethnographer and community (2002). Working towards building community identity and foregrounding histories in Milton Keynes, he was creating the re-enacting and inciting of culture which Alexander requires in performance ethnography: 'the performance of possibilities' (2005:431). The performances were 'offering reflexive insights to wide audiences ... mov[ing] participants towards being visible where previously they were not' which fulfils Mienczakowski's function of ethnodrama (1997:170). This is close to the purpose envisaged by anthropologist Elwyn C. Lapoint, who claims to have invented the term ethnodrama twenty five years ago, to 'gain the kinaesthetic experience of existence in another culture that broadens [researchers'] understanding in a way that traditional study cannot, and allows them, as much as is possible, to break out of the frame of reference they have inherited from their own culture'.

Nevitt was doing what is at the heart of the practice of this book, but the term ethnodrama was not used at the time, and he'd obviously not heard of Elwyn C. Lapoint. Perhaps part of the problem with so many terms connecting with ethnodrama is that terms do not remain static. New conceptualisations, practices and trends shove them about. We cannot ignore the transience of terms and labels. They shift and transmute and combine in different places and spaces.

Terms and their implications for practice

But is it just the terms that are different or could it also be the practice? Does the term performance ethnography or ethnodrama render the terms documentary and verbatim theatre superfluous? Do terms eclipse other terms, or do they actually describe distinct practices? How are the different terms selected? Could individuals have invested in particular terms and hence have interest in prolonging their usage?

A plethora of terms is used to describe performed research. But we have stumbled already! 'Performed research' assumes that research data is presented in performance. This doesn't capture the fact that performative research is often seen as a method of inquiry in itself. Alice's project constitutes both a process of research through a performative exploration and a mode of dissemination. Other common terms include: ethnodrama; ethno-drama; performance ethnography; ethnographic performance; performative research; performed research; performance and reflexive anthropology; ethno performance; ethnographic based performance art; docu-drama; documentary theatre; community theatre; theatre of fact; verbatim theatre; reader's theatre. And we could go on.

Saldaña has suggested 'research-based art' as an over-arching term since 'the forms are in service to the content' (2008:196). But, as noted above, Alice and Victor and Jumai used performance arts processes as a means to discover the content, so the forms were more a process of discovery of content than being a service to it. Peter Thomson has argued that all playwriting is research. Saldaña has suggested that all playwrights are ethnodramatists since they are tellers of research-based stories. Yet, we have not heard playwrights identifying themselves as ethnodramatists or performance ethnographers, and rarely as researchers. Perhaps beyond the academy their primary aim is different. Paget suggests that verbatim theatre is often oppositional to mainstream views since its principal motive is giving voice to the disenfranchised and those outside the mainstream (1987). What is identified as ethnographic performance is also beyond the mainstream. *The Laramie Project* (Kaufman, 2001) gave voice to what may have remained an invisible story, and attracted significant attention across the globe, but even this would not be identified as mainstream.

Academics and ethnographers frequently work away from the mainstream, and they are more likely to refer to their work with an 'ethno' label. This gives it its place in the academy and its credentials as a research paradigm. McColl (cited in Sallis, 2009) proposes that those who use the term 'ethnographic research' often do so in order to identify their work within the qualitative and/or the ethnographic data research model. However, those in the mainstream are not generally required to identify with these notions which are so fundamental in the higher education sector. The terms we use are often associated with the context in which we work. We use what has the right associations and the terms others use when doing similar work.

If labels are selected to match purposes or practices, what exactly shapes the choices? Perhaps specific meanings are drawn from the grammar of each term. Performed ethnography is an adjective followed by a noun, which suggests that the ethnography is prime and the performance subsidiary: the adjective 'performed' defines how the noun 'ethnography' is manifested. So this might describe a project where the designer is more of an ethnographer than a performer, or whose objective is to demonstrate that the ethnography is of significance. What happens when this is turned around? Ethnographic performance, again, is an adjective followed by a noun. Here the performance side is given precedence and dominance, being the noun. The ethnographic is a defining typological adjective, as above. So we might usefully choose our terms with a sense of what is leading the work. 'Performance ethnography' helps us out since the two are equally valued. The term is made up of two nouns implying equal status.

This grammatical exploration could be employed to interrogate the implications of the numerous terms identified above. But we would like to identify the significance of the use of a compound term; ethno-drama. The compound may suggest that neither is complete without the other. Hence a new and distinct phenomenon is described which values an intrinsic connectedness between ethnography and drama, and drama and ethnography. So we have the term ethnodrama in the sub-title of the book, born of our determination that neither ethnography nor drama should be leading our study. Some may argue that the diminutive version of ethnography (ethno) gives greater status to drama, and others, no doubt, could propose other compounds, such as ethnotheatre.

The family tree

Aftershocks by Paul Brown and the Workers' Cultural Action Committee (1993) is described by Brown as 'a piece of Verbatim Theatre'. There is general consensus that Verbatim Theatre is using the words of people to provide a text that is performed. All our case study contributors have used the words of living participants, mostly the words of others. But in Alice, with its autobiographical focus, it is the words of the researcher/ ethnographer/performers. Using real people's narratives seems to be crucial to all the terms identified above. Verbatim text could be at the heart of the family of practices that may be huddled under the title 'Performing Research'. Saldaña highlights the importance for ethnodramatists of scrupulously ensuring that spoken text is used without losing the intended meanings of the original speakers (1998). But if they are all using verbatim, why are new terms required? We can't argue that responsibility to the text is considered less by ethnodramatists than by those creating verbatim theatre.

Michael Anderson notes the connections between the verbatim theatre tradition and current performance ethnographic practices. He argues for performance ethnographers to learn from those who have been working creatively in verbatim theatre for years. 'While researchers' stock in trade has always been research (and not theatre), verbatim theatre practitioners have long been engaged in the aesthetic work of telling research stories to engage an audience' (2007:80). The assumption that the 'verbatim practitioners' are not researchers is interesting. Anderson's distinction seems to lie in a primary interest or motive: research versus theatrical communication to a live audience. Yet Linden's work reveals that what she calls verbatim theatre entails a gathering of data that may appropriately be described as research. Linden, who has been working on her MA, refers to research. Can this distinction be maintained? The motives for both are to give voice to untold stories, wishing to 'make a difference' (Madison, 2005:192), a 'moral discourse' (Alexander, 2005:417). So why might work be called verbatim theatre rather than ethnodrama or ethnographic performance? Whilst the use of verbatim aims and research activity may be common, it may be argued that verbatim theatre is perhaps less explicit about its research process, even perhaps less inclined to see the production process as part of the on-going research. Victor and Jumai use recorded narratives and yet also develop data through the performance workshop process. They do not refer to their work as verbatim. But they do, like Brown on *Aftershocks*, refer to documentary theatre.

Paget identifies oral history and documentary techniques in verbatim theatre (1987) and Anderson states that 'Verbatim theatre sits squarely within the documentary drama tradition' (2007:83). If verbatim is the heart of the family of practices, how should we view documentary theatre? Attilio Favorini traces documentary theatre back to 492BC when the Greek Phrynichus produced a play about the Persian War

24

(www.porteparole.org/doc-theatre). We understand it as theatre that tells of a real event, generally from documented information. It is related to Theatre of Fact, a term used in the past when there was more confidence in the certainty of facts. Theatre of Fact is associated with German playwrights such as Peter Weiss and Heiner Kipphardt, who were writing political plays to ensure the Second World War was not forgotten and urging that lessons be learnt. Their source materials included official documents and court records. It is often assumed that documentary theatre uses more than voices as its source materials, whereas verbatim is based solely on voices, but this may be a neater distinction in theory than in practice.

Many writers on performing research discuss the dilemma of moving real dialogue into dramatic form, and the case study contributors are no exceptions, as the following chapters show. All refer to the responsibility of having an individual's actual words, alongside the task of building a script. What is included and what omitted? What is placed next to what and what are the implications of this placing of text? Brown refers to *Aftershocks* as 'a fabrication, just like any drama spun from a writer's head' (1993:i) which suggests that verbatim cannot simply reproduce recorded voices without the creative act of creating performance from the lines that will engage an audience. Richard's work, like Victor and Jumai's, brings not only recorded narrative but additional data, gathered through activities such as observation and workshop experiences. It would be handy to make a distinction between documentary and verbatim practices with ethnodrama by saying that the former terms imply a more rigid allegiance to the words, but it is not so clear cut.

Paget describes ethnographic performance as a genre which is 'native, artful, subtle, imaginative, interpretive, and dialogical' (cited in Sallis, 2009). This sense of the dialogic is distinctive. Ethnographic practices 'might best be understood as a dialogue in which performers and audience engage in an equal exchange (Cozart *et al*, 2003:53). This focus on the possibility of dialogue is present in descriptions of ethnodrama and ethnographic performance and performance ethnography but appears less in descriptions of community theatre, theatre of fact, verbatim and documentary theatres. This does appear to identify a different branch in the family tree.

If the dialogic helps us to consider a distinction between some of the terms, how might ethnodrama, ethnographic performance/performance ethnography be distinguished from one another? Why do some people choose one term rather than another? For Denzin, performance ethnography is 'literally the staged re-enactment of ethnographically derived notes' (2003:41) and for Conquergood it is 'a way of knowing and a mode of understanding, as well as a method of critical inquiry' (1991:187). Is this really different from what is called ethnodrama? Looking at the literature it seems that those who see the performance development as a significant part of the research process are more likely to describe their work as ethnographic performance or performance ethnography than those who see the performance as the presentation of research data completed prior to the performance planning. In our case studies, Alice and Victor and Jumai's contributions speak of the whole process as their research and refer to their work as performance ethnography. The Hong Kong performances, with their time constraint, clearly identify the performance planning as making decisions about how best to present their research data, rather than how the planning process will develop further data, and they use the term ethnodrama. Furthermore, the literature suggests that those who have an education background and use their work in a pedagogic context appear to favour the term ethnodrama. This may be because some have made a connection between ethnographic performance work and drama and theatre in education (eg Mienczakowski, 1994).

In conclusion

There are many related practices with similar aims and interests which share some approaches, such as using 'verbatim'. It may be that there are differences in context and hence terminology, and assumptions about the various labels. There are also some distinctions in motives, sometimes resulting in different practices. In this book, by including case studies which use different terms to describe their work, we are clearly not seeking to be exclusive. Indeed, the title of the book was subject to extensive discussion. We hope that the title expresses that our interest lies in the practice of performing research and our recognition that this comes in different shapes and under different labels.

3
RESPONSIBILITIES

The need for this chapter was foreshadowed in Chapter 1, as we began to explore the manifold and diverse purposes of the various participants in ethnodrama: the researchers, the re-searched communities and the audiences, and how their purposes intersect, interact, and sometimes don't do either very well. The need becomes more insistent when we frame those purposes inside a bigger question so far untackled: what's the purpose of research itself? What is research for, and how does our particular paradigm of ethnodrama fit into that?

This question was brought sharply into focus for one of the authors during a recent dinner-time conversation, when he innocently dropped into the discussion the phrase 'creative research'. That was enough for a simultaneous squawk of disbelief and protest from two other guests, who both fervently maintained that being creative was absolutely no business of research, and if it was creative, then it wasn't research. The job of research was to establish what could be established: 'finding out the truth' as one of them asserted. This was a red rag, to the author and the several artists and educators round the table. The truth-merchant's friend qualified that assertion by redefining it as 'taking pains and find-ing out the facts'. The subsequent arguments raised against them came from a range of sometimes warring perspectives which they themselves label 'constructivist', 'phenomenological', 'post-structuralist' and 'post-post-modern'. These warriors came together to proclaim the com-plexity of human behaviour, notions of provisional, ephemeral, changing and subjective truths, and phrases like 'mapping ambiguity' and 're-constructing realities'. All of this cut little ice with the dissenters. That one of the protesters was a computer engineer and the other a veterinarian partly explains their trenchantly positivistic outlook, and the whole table quickly agreed that ambiguous computer software or provisional and ephemeral dog tablets would be irresponsible in the extreme. Their next question, however, hung in the air unresolved: 'Is what you people do responsible?' ... and the hosts quickly moved the conversation elsewhere before serious acrimony set in.

Fortunately, the academic battle to recognise in research the subjective, ambiguous and dynamic nature of human social behaviour, and the possibility of multiple and even conflicting truths, has been won in the last twenty years. It has, at least, within the universities, in the humanities, the arts and in places within the social sciences, though there are plenty of psychologists and sociologists around who still have no interest in a phenomenon unless they can pin it down and measure it. This does not mean that our scientists' piquant question can be ignored. Acknowledging subjectivity is not the same thing at all as 'anything goes', and the permission to take liberties with appearances, and bring creativity into the discourse, brings much greater responsibilities. We may never get it all right (whatever 'it' happens to be), but we can still get it wrong, and getting it wrong can mislead, distress, disempower, create destructive misunderstandings and wreak conflict in the real world of the communities we are investigating.

The authors started sketching out this chapter with the notion that the word power must be central to the discussion – Who holds the power? Who doesn't? Power to do what? In a sense it is central but power is also a vague word, so we are breaking it down loosely into discussion of four important dimensions:

- social responsibility
- ethics
- representation and misrepresentation
- gatekeepers and constraints

Much of this relates to the discussion started in the previous chapter, and these four headings also overlap.

Social responsibility ... and social action

It is noticeable and not accidental that most ethnodramas are generated within professions where social responsibility either to specified groups or to some greater social good is *de rigueur*: education, health and human services. One of our case study writers, Kate from Hong Kong, expressed this apologetically in terms of where she started in her own ethnodramatic journey, as a student setting out to document and perform the lives of local scrap pickers. She acknowledged that she was just doing an academic exercise with no purpose for the researcher/performers beyond the educational. Kate and her colleagues were aware of how easily they could be perceived by both the informants and their social workers as dilettantes in an area of grave social concern where research might be expected to be conducted with the aim of alleviating their plight.

In this she is probably not doing her social instincts justice, for there must have been some reason why the group chose to represent the lives of scrap pickers. Her colleague Will became interested in using their project to help build understanding and care between different communities in his society. Cautiously, Richard Sallis makes a similar point that an underlying aim of his project was to ascertain the benefit ... the 'usefulness' of an ethnographic performance written as part of an educational ethnography.

Will's and Richard's motivation echoes the strong thread of social purpose evident in the literature. Jim Mienczakowski constantly reiterates it in terms of creating 'theatre of change':

> We intend to be both descriptive and insightful but above all useful and explanatory. In order to do this we interpret other people to ourselves. (1994:50)

> If we are very lucky, the audiences and performers of performed ethnography leave the room or the auditorium changed in some way (1997:166).

This social educational responsibility resonates with Victor and Jumai's purpose, to 'broaden understanding' specifically 'to contest the stereotypical misrepresentation of black people in British history'. Victor and Jumai go further towards resolving an apparent paradox, which is why ethnodrama, the specific study and performance of one single community that by definition cannot be 'typed' or generalised outwards, will 'broaden understanding'. But that's the point: its specificity can, they claim, help to counter the dangers of reductionism and the need to avoid generalisations about the experiences and histories of black people – especially as British history has been reductionist to the point of diminishing and erasing black people and their contributions to UK society.

In other words, the misleading generalisations are already out there, and the specificity of a piece of ethnodrama subverts or at least challenges such generalisations and stereotyping.

Another phrase of Mienczakowski's hints at a grander purpose still:

> Ethnodramas...it is their overt intention not just transgressively to blur boundaries but to be a form of public voice ethnography that has emancipatory and educational potential. (2001:469)

This is somewhat disingenuous, since this discussion comes in a passage where he is not blurring boundaries at all but policing firm distinctions between ethnodrama and other similar forms such as verbatim theatre. His use of the word 'emancipatory' implies more than just freeing the understanding, and leads to another set of possibilities, which have been enthusiastically embraced by the community of ethnographers: not just changing understanding, but proactively using ethnodrama as social action, to change society. The idea of ethnodrama as social action is a concept which we asked some of our case study writers to explore and interrogate in their own accounts. It's an idea which would have our engineer and vet going into an even sharper decline, so in fairness to them we need to take some of the claims that are made with a deal of salt. The claims in the academic literature range, sometimes in the same writings, from the modest:

> The collaborative power of performance and ethnography utilizes an embodied aesthetic practice coupled with the descriptive knowledge of lives and the conditions of living to stir up and provoke audiences to a critical social realisation and possible response (Alexander, 2005:411).

through the analytical:

> The potential lies in revealing issues of who gets to speak and for whom... How participants choose to maintain or disrupt the perceptual stasis that exists ... such attempts seek to frame performance as a critical and reflexive agency that initiates action (*ibid*:411-412).

to the apocalyptic:

> For some, the notion of overthrowing structures of oppression might seem far-fetched and beyond the scope of traditional ethnography, yet theories and practices in performance studies and theater arts have been moving steadily towards the social and political goals of using performance as a tool and method of social change ... such attempts seek to frame performance as a critical and reflexive agency that initiates action (*ibid*:412).

Alexander's vision of a brave new world is endorsed by the doyen of ethnography, Norman Denzin, an equally enthusiastic supporter of ethnodrama. Not only do 'Ethnodramas help create the conditions for an emancipatory democratic politics' (Denzin and Lincoln 2006:xi), but

> Ethnotheatre is a manifesto that exposes oppression and challenges the existing social order through an artistic rendering of moral and political discourse. (Denzin 2004, in Saldaña 2005:3)

... and much the same in many other of his writings over the last decade.

There is a vein of ethnodrama, and particularly auto-ethnographic performance, whose practitioners take statements like these as their battle-cry, and take on society with the aim at the very least, as Alexander puts it, 'to stir up and provoke audiences to a critical social realisation and possible response' (2005:411). The titles of their books boldly proclaim their polemic: *I speak from the wound in my mouth* (Weems, 2002), or *Fires in the mirror* (Smith, 1993), and their contents are often incendiary to match.

Not all the literature is so shrill, however, and many researcher-performers do have a social change agenda just because they have come to ethnodrama as educators, part of whose educational purpose may not be to change the world, but just some of the attitudes in a small bit of it, such as

> The inclusion of multiple voices and perspectives allows for more points of recognition for audience members, thus helping to normalize their experiences, and also extending the meanings that can be created and derived from illness. Productions like *Handle with care?* provide practising health professionals with an opportunity to reconnect, in deep ways, with the issues facing ill people. Research-based drama can also be an extraordinary vehicle for training health professionals ... It takes audiences beyond a preoccupation with techniques and goals, to an empathic experience with the ill

person. It is exactly such empathy that is arguably the precondition for trans-formation of health care ... to make a positive difference outside academia, in clinical and community settings. (Gray *et al*, 2000:143).

A hunch that research-based drama might be such 'an extraordinary vehicle for training health professionals' and that it might just work, is what got Jill Robinson involved in her case study in this book, for exactly the same reasons as the writers above. She wanted to use the script in the classroom with health professional students, in order for health professionals to learn to empathise with the experiences of others. Perhaps in the classroom students should be given opportunities to en-gage their humanity and identify with human experience in a personal and embodied way.

For Victor and Jumai, too, more than any other of our contributors, an agenda of social action through education was a driving force. For them history is not only implicated in politics, the narrative is a contested site and whoever controls it, shapes how a people's history is presented and perceived. Therefore, among their aims were: to offer alternative narra-tives about the 'histories' of black presence in Northampton and to counter negative images of black people through an objective inter-rogation of their experiences and place in multicultural Britain.

Ethics

Ethnographic researcher/performers are often preoccupied by ethics and explicit about them in much the same way as they are about social issues and responsibilities: they work in fields like education, health and human services. For those involved in the human ethics com-mittees which vet projects, as well as for the researchers/performers themselves, ethnodrama is both good and bad news.

For its strongest adherents the very act of ethnodrama is a positive matter of ethical choice closely connected with social responsibility. The power and potency of ethnographic performance contains a moral imperative: that it must, in Denzin's words: 'awaken moral sensibility. It must move the other and the self to action' (1997:xxi). The ethical res-ponsibilities of ethnodrama are one area which has already received considerable debate and discussion within the literature. Johnny Saldaña (1998) candidly reveals, and thoroughly discusses as a 'confessional tale', the many-sided ethical dilemmas he faced in his early ethnodrama *Maybe someday, if I'm famous*, which were obvious to members of his audience, including both the authors of this book. As the performance of the ethnodrama was at a large conference of drama educators, the discussion resonated among workers in drama and research for some years, including contributions from Helen Nicholson (1999:102) who didn't buy the confession and remained confused, and Jim Mienczakowski (1999:99) who largely exonerated Saldaña's decision making – 'Well, that's showbiz, folks'.

Mienczakowski's response is endorsed in part, at least for the case studies in this book, by the experience of our contributor Jill, who initially wanted to hurry away and remove the most emotionally challenging dialogue from her script. She was discouraged from doing this by her colleagues and the group of students themselves. They challenged the presumption that an intense emotional response was the wrong response and therefore unethical.

For ourselves, the inherent ethical issues in Saldaña's well-ploughed ethnodrama form a small but important aspect of another major problem which all ethnodramas face, of which Saldaña is more aware than most. These are the inevitable tensions between art-making and the gathering and reporting of research, and will be dealt with in detail in Chapter 4.

Jim Mienczakowski constantly reinforces the responsibilities of researchers to their community and its witnesses to report faithfully and, particularly in the case of vulnerable respondents, as Hippocrates put it: 'first, do no harm'. Mienczakowski's absolution of Saldaña's 'ethical angst' (1999:97) is perhaps untypical. He and his team tend to take the high moral ground and have even produced 'a set of guidelines to assist health theatre producers incorporate ethical and responsible standards into their ethnodrama' (Mienczakowski *et al* 1999:43), and they make bombing raids on work they regard as unethical, both in the literature (*ibid*:49) and in real life, precipitating the cancellation of a national tour of a piece of young people's theatre which did not come up to their standards (Brown, 1998).

Nowadays no research project in human social behaviour in a university gets ethics clearance without the most rigorous scrutiny. The same tight scrutiny is not applied to kindred forms like commercial docu-drama and verbatim theatre. Reinforcing the link between these and ethnodrama, Johnny Saldaña poses the intriguing suggestion that 'all playwrights are ethnodramatists' (2005:4).

> Debate continues on the tension between an ethnodramatist's ethical obliga-tion to recreate an authentic representation of reality (thus enhancing fidelity), and the licence for artistic interpretation of that reality (thus enhanc-ing the aesthetic possibilities). (*ibid*:32)

Rigorous scrutiny has not always been universal in the colleges and universities. This gives us the opportunity to consider a case study, safely protected by the passage of considerable time, of this particular issue of the tension between ethics and aesthetics. The problem arose twice in a very early ethnodrama which one of the authors, John, was involved with in 1981. This was well before John had heard of the word ethnodrama and maybe before it was invented, though the play, as it was then simply called, certainly has all the hallmarks we have identi-fied in Chapter 2.

Using our contemporary terminology, the ethnographic performers be-hind *Get Thee to a Nunnery* were a group of drama students who had decided that they were interested in finding out about the lives of con-temporary Christian nuns and putting on a play about them to their friends and fellow students. The word 'research' didn't figure as part of the grand design but as playwrights they knew they had to research their subject and with sensitivity and integrity, reinforcing Saldaña's suggestion. Unfortunately the secular and sceptical student researchers and their limited data sources led to a build-up of very negative data, much of it derived from people's memories of unhappy and barbaric schooldays. They were acquiring plenty of vivid, poetic and potentially dramatic material, but the play was heading towards a savage attack on nuns, as this extract of transcript indicates:

> Immediately what I think of when anybody asks me about nuns – I think of the vows of poverty and charity they take on... I think of the huge lack of charity one sees in a nun. After twelve years of schooling with them I sup-pose what I think of immediately is Sister Loretta Maria – who absolutely terrorised the fifth grade class. She had this sort of huge body, she was about six-foot two and was Irish, she had wild blue eyes – I'm sure one of them was

a glass eye. She had a gold tooth in the front of her mouth, and she was really the fiercest thing we had ever seen, and she just terrorised us. She used to walk behind us, and punch you in the back for no particular reason... one of my friends, Angela Atkinson, used to wet her pants constantly as this fierce creature walked past – she just had to stand beside her and she wet her pants. I don't know why we didn't go home and tell them, but a nun was a nun. She was Christ's bride if you are a catholic family, and there can't be anything wrong with Christ's bride (names changed).

This was marvellous raw material dramatically but not exactly even-handed and most of what the researchers gathered was in this vein. What sympathetic witness they found tended to be pedestrian or low-key, like some well-meaning but very lame poems about her life, generously provided by a nun. Those poems also provided the team with the first tension between the ethical and the aesthetic. Should these sincere, deeply felt and mawkish verses be used, at the risk of being counter-productive to their author's and the playwrights' intention, in the ears of a sceptical and literate audience? In this tension the ethical and aesthetic dilemmas were hand in hand: the ethical problem was a result of the aesthetic one. Before the team had decided how to handle this poser, they were confronted by one where ethics and aesthetics were in direct opposition, a problem which would define whether the play survived or fell on each count.

A student we will call Elaine had an aunt who was a reclusive Carmelite nun and this woman agreed to be interviewed by her niece. Disappointingly, the Mother Superior flatly refused to let Elaine make a tape recording. The student duly made notes as best she could, but when she brought them back to the research team, they were rather flat. Little of substance came out of the interview other than that her aunt liked the life and felt at peace. However, the naughty girl had hidden a tape recorder in her handbag, which she played to the team, who collectively gasped as they listened quite improperly to a monologue of eloquent beauty, full of substance in the softly spoken language and cadences of the speaker, where the gentle nun's sincerity of calling and devotion shone through the words she chose and the pitch and tone of her voice. She described the life in words and tones that Elaine could not have written down, but which the researcher-actors could absorb and to some degree re-create. The words themselves are vivid though they were only a small part of the experience that Elaine had witnessed and the students were sharing through directly hearing it:

I'll never forget the joy I felt when I first walked into my little cell – ah, I thought, now I'm home. It was the most beautiful little cell, lovely white-washed walls, and you're there by yourself with God alone. Oh, it was really lovely. It's really true – when you enter, God treats you gently. God calls each one differently, but, you know, it's just like – you know – when you want to get married, God puts deep within you... and different things that happen in your life lead to that... it's not a sad life at all – it's just – I can't explain it; it's because it's what God wants you to do. You're happy in it. You're so happy... I know God loves me and that God will – even as a child this came to me – that God will never let me down. Ordinary people can let me down, but God? Never. We just go on day by day, and God's grace is there every day.

The students' dilemma was ethical, intellectual and artistic. They had no right to listen to it, let alone use it; yet only by using it could they provide a remotely fair or authentic picture of their subjects. They could also provide a much better balanced artwork, where the positive and negative images could counterpoint each other vividly and drama-tically. These tensions will be discussed further in Chapter 5. To com-plicate the matter, the witness herself, as a reclusive nun, would not be an audience to the final piece and in those days the idea of member-checking data was not part of the game. As usual, there were also other extraneous but crucial factors: they could not abandon the project since it was academic course work and assessment depended on the project's completion. Moreover, most of their other witnesses were waiting expectantly to see how the researcher-performers had treated their commentary. Whatever they did, the project was hopelessly com-promised. And so are we, having shared it with you readers. And of course, so are you, now you have read it.

Nowadays the ethical policing of student work and all research makes this scenario much less likely to happen. Students police themselves, like those represented in this book such as Richard, who was very mind-ful that there could be personal and professional repercussions for the teachers and their students when the play was made public. So he be-gan his research project with a set of unwritten, yet commonly under-stood ethical principles which he negotiated with the two teachers involved to help ensure that the perspectives of the participants were respected and appropriately represented.

No less cautious, Will from Hong Kong nevertheless found the dilemma itself challenging and exhilarating. On the one hand he felt that his own team's ethnodrama did not solve the question of whether drama can still educate and entertain at the same time as it ethically, honestly and accurately reports research. He found from his project experience and his reading that the two dimensions put certain limitations on each other. Nevertheless the experience did not daunt his confidence in the form and he concluded that given a better design and arrangement, each dimension could support the other and 'bring about wonderful effects'.

In his scrupulously ethical approach to his ethnodrama, Richard took one precaution which was not typical of the others in the book except Linden – though she had different reasons. His dialogue would all be quoted verbatim from what was recorded in the field, either from observation or interview. Moreover, the words and actions of the participants would not be imaginatively re-worked to the extent that they were unrecognisable from the general context in which they originated. This collides interestingly with Victor and Jumai's decision to fictionalise events and characters in order to avoid falling foul of copyright legislation and ethical issues. They believe the work is still authentic and reflects the histories of black peoples. However, the subjective, personal, and biographical voices give way to the objectification of those voices. Fiction and fictionalising can be a double-edged sword in this field. Richard's intention was to protect his respondents by honouring their input to the letter; Victor and Jumai's was to protect them by transforming it.

In Moises Kaufman's famous and commercially successful ethnodrama *The Laramie Project* (2001) the Tectonic Theatre team knew from the start the ethical minefield they were treading, investigating a homophobic murder in the community in which it happened and bringing that to the public stage. How they traversed the minefield, and occasionally set off mines that blew up in their faces, forms a partially explicit and intensely implicit strand of the narrative of the play itself: they display the shrapnel.

There is one aspect of the ethics of this well-debated piece, which was acclaimed artistically, that has not been fully addressed. Part of the argument for the integrity and honour of the company, and therefore the ethical justification of this play, was that the theatre team were explicit, both with the Laramie community in the research itself, and in the performance, about their role. One layer of the narrative was their own story of the research and its predicaments as told and as played by themselves. That seemed fine when we saw it in New York, played by the Tectonic Theatre Company, because they also brought a performance style which limpidly displayed their integrity. The company had also considered and dealt as sensitively as they could with one significant audience factor: that in this performance they were placing the audience in the role of voyeurs, complicit in being entertained by the private anguish and grief, viciousness and prejudice of a real-life community, some of whom had refused to sanction it. Whether that is ever ethically justifiable is a debate which is far wider than ethnodrama; it applies, and is being contested, right across fields such as documentary drama and film, reality TV and neighbouring genres like verbatim theatre.

More recently, we saw *The Laramie Project* in Sydney, produced and performed by a director and actors who were nothing to do with the original performing team and therefore completely uninvolved in the research team. Nor of course could they have that team's limpid integrity in performance. How might the people of Laramie consider this? What position does it put the director and actors in? It's certainly a far cry from the relationship which the Tectonic Theatre team had with their informants and the whole real-life Laramie catastrophe. So what position does this put the audience in, where the whole experience is gratuitous to a degree that the New York audiences might comfort themselves that theirs was not... Or was it?

4

OWNERSHIP AND POWER

Notions of authority, faithfulness and adaptation

Whether in the form of a film or a book, or whether an account must be condensed to a paragraph or fills a 300-page monograph, we must still be accountable for the consequences of our representations and the implications of our messages – because they matter. (Madison, 2005:5)

The voices of our case study writers express concern for doing what is right by the participants through their ethnodramas. There are repeated references to wishing to give the 'truth' of what the participants had explained, to be 'faithful' to those individuals and to be 'honouring the data'. Getting an appropriate representation of their research data certainly mattered to them. This is hardly surprising given the notion that performance ethnography is deemed a 'moral discourse' (Alexander, 2005:417) and the responsibility to others is emphasised by those who express concern about the possibility of such work given the potential for colonising the 'other' (Bacon, 2006:136).

Representing the research findings accurately in performance is difficult, as is representing them in written research reports, as we have seen in Chapter 1. Perhaps being 'accountable' for our work, as Madison urges, is as good as it gets, though it is still no simple feat. This implies a moral imperative to aim at being most true and to feel comfortable about justifying the decisions that have been made. Even with the best of intentions, there are still challenges. After all, what is a true, authentic, honest and honouring representation? Richard states that ethnodramatists share a view that theatrical writing/presentation is an appropriate way to tell the real stories of others and we shall consider some of the challenges to being true in the telling of those stories and to ensuring that they are appropriately told.

Lack of participant homogeneity

The first problem with trying to be faithful to participant stories is that there is unlikely to be homogeneity amongst the participant groups. What might appear to be an honest portrayal of a community to one participant may not be for another. The specificity of ethnodrama projects helps, but within a single drama class in Richard's site, a range of people connected by a train accident in different ways in Linden's, and four academics in Alice's there is a difference in how actions are understood and interpreted and how life is experienced. Which interpretation is the researcher to follow in the cause of truth when differences are evident? Do sacrifices have to be made to avoid muddying the overall narrative?

Some of our ethnodramatist case study writers found themselves considering whether all views should be presented equally. The group working with the data about Indonesian maids in Hong Kong felt they shouldn't include extremes. Elaine explains how they scrutinised every piece of data carefully. Then they avoided words that were emotional, especially from quotations taken from the abused maids and social workers they interviewed. Another team member explained that the team always took care to counterbalance a statement or comment made in a performance and make sure that the viewpoints of the maids and the employers were both presented. The group, working within a tight time frame for a Masters Degree assessment, did not have the opportunity to bring the participants together, and it might have been difficult to encourage two such groups to discuss the points together. But, this would be the next step to begin a journey of learning and change. Perhaps one group would have felt their views were more sympathetically or fully expressed in the performance than the others'. So the resolution of how to be true to all the views was to keep a balance.

While the balance created is a way to deal with the desire to ensure that the voices of all participants are equally heard, perhaps it compromises the didactic spirit of ethnodrama. If ethnodrama is to bring about transformation and social change, should, or how should, the views of the employers who have been abusing the Indonesian maids be expressed? Should all participants' views be represented equally? Mienczakowski (1994) states that in ethnodrama the conclusions are left to the discretion of the audience, as we shall consider below. Should both positions be equally presented so that the audience can make their own decisions? Some might assume a position in which the employers should not be judged for believing they are justified in abusing maids who do not do things the way they want them done. However, those who hold with a view that there are certain absolutes regarding right and wrong and basic human rights may not wish the employers' attitudes to be given equal status. It may also be a question of how the view is presented. Many a radical playwright has given a political view without exploring the 'other' view. They know we do not wish to go to see a performance to be preached at, so rather than a single view, we see plots designed to undermine particular behaviours or lampoon 'other' views. Ultimately, we know the political view that will be expressed if we are going to see certain writers' work, such as a David Hare or Bertolt Brecht play, but they will consider how to effect their political questions or messages.

The British Broadcasting Corporation (BBC) has a mission to present the news in a neutral way. This often means giving a range of different views. Studies explore the biases identified through the framing of the news items. Even at a basic level, which side is presented first will affect the way news is interpreted. Stuart Hall refers to 'primacy' to explain how one side's view may be given first and then the other is positioned not to present their case, but to answer the charges as set up by the first view. Hence the former has primacy while the second is disadvantaged. An example Hall presents is in a strike the employers are given primacy, being interviewed first, seen in an office (which gives status) and they are invited to state the issues. They focus on the risks of the strike, such as the damage to the economy. The strikers are not then asked to present their case, but to answer to the charges made already by the employers. They are filmed on the picket lines giving an unruly, perhaps scary impression to the viewers. (Hall *et al*, 1978) So the BBC, with a mandate to present neutrally, is seen to present bias when dealing with different viewpoints. Similarly, the ethnographer will present through imbalance, perhaps unconsciously as well as consciously.

The ethnodramatists also negotiate to what degree they seek balance and how they might use views to deliver their identified aims for the piece. Underlying the desire to respect the differing participant voices are the aims of the project. When the researchers' overall aim is for the project to communicate something in particular, it may be that being true to the research participants is compromised: there is tension between being true to the participants and being true to the project's intentions.

It is also a problem when participants wish to put over a particular view in their story for their own purposes. This sometimes arises with work with organisations and publically run agencies. The teachers in Richard's project were open and supportive but must clearly have kept an eye on how their drama work would be publically presented, as any of us in that professionally challenging situation would do. Richard had extensive discussion with the school students about how their contributions were to be presented. Some students were keen to have their own lines of dialogue explicitly associated with themselves rather than have the originator of the lines unrecognisable. It is those students whose words feature significantly in the play who seemed keen to be identified. They were clearly thinking about how they wished to have their image presented; in a sense these boys were making decisions beyond what was best for the play. They were thinking about how they and their comments would be perceived. This is inevitable when participants are genuinely invited to share in the process in the open way facilitated by Richard. But this may complicate the endeavour to find consensus about how the research site tells its stories. Jill identifies a poignant moment when an exchange about certain practices between the health professionals and parents who were the research participants in her project exemplified the different versions of reality and truth that were held by the two groups. So if there are many truths, can they all be represented?

Linden talks of feeling conflict between the 'risk of authenticity' and her responsibility for the audience. Initially, she acknowledges that much of the interest in the play she produced is directly attributable to the authentic voice of its content. People were excited by the fact that the play was telling real people's stories. She wished to keep to verbatim speech, to be faithful to those who had spoken to her, sharing their experiences of something painful. However, a member of an early audience found a part of her performance distressing and didn't feel that it should have been included. Yet, by including the part, Linden was presenting exactly what another participant had wanted or perhaps needed to see. This is another dilemma for the ethnodramatist: are the interests of the audience to be taken into account as much as those of the participants and the ethnodramatist? Considering the audience, as in this example, may have implications for the degree to which faithfulness to the research data can be maintained. Questions centre on what is appropriate for an audience to witness and who is being protected and who put at risk.

On the other hand, having no different views might also pose a problem. If a range of positions or attitudes are not presented in the project, the single view can emerge as a hero or victim narrative, or a moral crusade, or perhaps even a moral tirade. There may be a time when to avoid this, some distance is required from the authenticity of the participants' stories. When I, Judith, watched *Alice Hoy is Not a Building*, I laughed with recognition at the struggles of combining a family and a career in higher education. But deep down, I wanted to see an alternative to the women struggling and feeling overwhelmed. I yearned to see the woman who didn't need to stand on a chair for her mobile to work, who did get her class moved into better rooms, who felt in command and control, and who did stop the department from cutting drama and who didn't need to hurry down the corridor to get to the crucial meeting! I wanted her to be in time to have a coffee first. Both male and female co-editors loved the piece but we both wanted, or maybe needed, another voice. Yet our voices are not those of the researchers in their auto-ethnography. As ever, this may say as much about the audience members as the performance.

So in 'honouring the data', the responsibility of the ethnodramatist is not only to consider the different views of the participants and weigh them up against the interests of the audience but also to ensure that the piece moves beyond mono-messages. This is in addition to maintaining the overall aim of the project. It is through recognising these competing demands and identifying appropriate compromises that ethnodramatists may become fully accountable for their work.

Position and the choosing of dialogue

In the struggle to achieve a faithful presentation of the research data and the participants' voices, ethnodramatists are engaging with more than the views of their participants. Their own positions inevitably drift into the frame, despite their oft expressed commitment not to bring their own attitudes and opinions to the work.

Now there is a greater awareness that identity and the notion that this is not a simple or singular noun will influence how we perceive the world and report on our findings. As researchers we must consider that it is crucial who we are when we ask questions and assess how much we can empathise with the views of those with different identities and in different cultural contexts. At the International Drama in Education Research Institute in 2003, women in the Feminist Methodology research group found great difficulty obtaining genuine responses in their interviews with men. The group was clearly identified as full of women who were critical of men, so gender identities got in the way of the research process.

Winnie from Hong Kong identifies the difficulty here, admitting that although they tried their best to avoid value judgment on an issue, it was not possible to be one hundred per cent clear. Lena, who was working on a DINKs (double income no kids) project recognised the seepage of personal opinions. She acknowledged that at the beginning of the research, she had a purpose to change the perception of some DINKs, but that after the whole process, she recognised that she had gained more respect towards DINKs and their choice. In this case the project brought about a conceptual change for the researcher with an open and reflexive approach. Hence, the personal opinion may have impacted at an early stage but not by the end of the project. Another case study writer suggested that she could take a neutral position because she had not experienced the particular context being explored but the innocent view is unfortunately not possible. The lack of direct experience does not halt any of us from having views. Can a project then not have the views of the researchers somehow interlaced with the real stories of the researched community? Can we subdue our own opinions and agendas in the endeavour to be faithful – and indeed should we?

There must be a selection process about which dialogue will be used and this is inevitably dictated by the ethnodramatist. But in terms of authenticity and remaining true to the data, our ethnographers found issues about the emotional content. Jill explains that after she witnessed the impact on the first students who performed a reading of her script, she wanted to hurry away and remove the most emotionally challenging dialogue from the script. However, she was discouraged from doing so by colleagues and her students themselves, who challenged her presumption that an intense emotional response was the wrong response. The level of emotional response and consequential increase in empathy which the student health professionals need to serve and support the parents better emerged as a significant positive in the achievement of a project aim. But including the emotional dialogue also maintains faithfulness to the narratives.

Of course, emotional dialogue is also helpful dramatically. In his initial longer draft, Richard wishes to avoid what Saldaña describes as the 'juicy' bits (1998:181) merely for the sake of dramatic engagement. However, there may be an issue about the term 'juicy' here. It assumes an exploitative, gratuitous approach. If instead we referred to using emotionally challenging content for the sake of being properly accountable for the work, we would feel more comfortable. Richard's use of the term 'merely' is weighted due to his admirable commitment to the research data. The tensions between the aesthetic and responsibility to the data are considered in Chapter 5. In our attempt to be faithful to the narratives given, we need to consider emotional content. How it is presented will determine whether or not audiences and participants see it as 'juicy' or authentic, though there may not be agreement, as in Linden's example.

Awareness of our own positioning and how it interacts with the participants' contributions, is of key importance, given the responsibility the ethnodramatist carries, 'because it matters'. The influence brought to bear beyond the research participants will be considered further in the 'Gatekeepers and power' section later in this chapter.

Verbatim and characters

It is said that drama is life with the boring bits left out. Ethnodramatists often feel a tug of duty to be faithful and don't wish to exclude what they might see as the boring bits when they may not be the boring bits to the participant. Deciding whether to use the data verbatim or whether to alter it for the performance causes ethnodramatists considerable anxiety. A sense of guilt for changes and additions emerges, but also recognition that it might actually be required not only for performance considerations but to give a clear depiction of the research site. Linden set out determined to use only verbatim but explains that

> ...as verbatim text moves towards theatrical production from research data, questions about its authenticity become increasingly frequent...I certainly found that over the entire arc of the verbatim theatre journey I became more flexible both in terms of what was said and who said it.

However, she found that 'some narratives were lost or diluted...but the work became more precise'.

Here ethnodramatists are caught up with ethical considerations. Many of the case study ethnographers share their decision-making processes about whether to keep characters according to the voices who gave the dialogue or whether to blend the dialogue to create compound, hybrid characters. Inherent in the dilemma is at one extreme the need to be loyal to the data and at the other, the need to protect the source of the script. Richard had plans that any dialogue would be 'quoted verbatim from what was recorded in the field' but he would create 'composite' characters to protect identities. However, the students in his participant group felt that the class members knew who said what anyway, and so composites were superfluous.

Jill describes how she amalgamated transcripts, bringing narrative from different people into a range of characters. She saw this as essential to protect the participants' identities. She also ventured from direct faithfulness in not revealing the children's specific diagnoses. The case studies demonstrate a range of considerations that impact on how the narratives might best be developed to remain faithful, although being faithful is not always achieved through the direct recreation of what was found in the research site. Some choices are made for the aesthetic rationale but not all. The aesthetic tensions raised by decisions about whether or not to use verbatim text are analysed in more detail in the next chapter.

Beyond verbatim

Achieving a truthful presentation of research data is not only determined by the text included. It has been suggested that dialogue accounts for only 35 per cent of communication in theatre, as in real-life interactions. The remaining 65 per cent is through other aspects of the semiotic process, such as facial expression, gesture, the space between performers, and costume. The account of the difference found between the transcript of a nun's story of her life and a recording of her telling her story, in the previous chapter, highlights just the oral side of this additional layer that the ethnodramatist must consider. The voice, its energy, tone, pitch and pace, as well as the pauses, gave a very different sense of the nun and her experience of living as a nun. The original notes of the interview had aroused little interest among the student researchers but the voice enthralled them. The way even single words are delivered can change the meaning entirely, if you think of just the ways 'no' might be delivered. So the journey from transcript to delivery is considered in the endeavour to remain as close to the research site as possible. Thought is given to exactly how something was expressed and what was meant by the participant's emphasis on certain words.

'...Representing others is always going to be a complicated and contentious undertaking' (Madison 2005:3-4) and even the tiniest gestures require analysis. Natalie described the anxiety of deciding how a girl should look in a piece about slimming culture in Hong Kong. The character was dancing and her tummy would come into view while she danced. Natalie mused that a slight smile on the girl's face would change the meaning. Her expression at this moment would be critical. One of the authors is currently involved in a project involving four monologues given by police officers from ethnic minority groups. They constitute part of a piece that uses humour to raise questions. The monologues were derived from research interviews and were to be the key emotional impact side to the work (as Saldaña would say: 'juicy'). The professional actors performing the monologues do not convey the hurt that the research participants expressed. They did not hear the real voices and are perhaps outside the experience. The stories are shocking. The script is there but this presentation has not honoured the narratives of those participants. Madison's point that we must be accountable for the consequences of our representations and the implications of our messages is crucial: every detail is relevant to the expression of a real person's story. In giving dignity to the participants' stories, the voices, tones, costumes and gestures are all relevant.

Adaptation theory

Adaptation theory provides frameworks through which to examine adaptations from one genre to another critically, usually from written text to visual genres. Issues concerning authenticity and faithfulness to the original are contested by different theorists.

There is a view that an adaptation creates a version of a source text with something new emerging.

> ...the best adaptations of books for film can often be approached as an activity of literary criticism, not a pictorialisation of the complete novel, but a critical essay which stresses what it sees as the main theme. Like a critical essay, the film adaptation selects some episodes, excludes others, offers preferred alternatives. It focuses on specific areas of the novel and has imaginative flights about some characters. In the process, like the best criticism, it can throw new light on the original. (Sinyard, 1986:117)

Victor and Jumai's work develops beyond the original transcripts and creates something new since the participants in the performance are also interacting with the data. They include young peoples' perspectives, although the original data was drawn from mature voices. Like the film adapter, the ethnodramatist is selecting particular aspects to include and inevitably producing 'preferred alternatives'. The issue of proximity to the text is as much an issue in adaptation as it is to the ethnodramatist.

> There are probably two basic approaches to the whole question of adaptation. The first approach asks that the integrity of the original work – the novel, say – be preserved, and therefore that it should not be tampered with and should in fact be uppermost in the adapter's mind. The second approach feels it proper and in fact necessary to adapt the original work freely, in order to create – in the different medium that is now being employed – a new, different work of art with its own integrity. (Beja cited in Giddings, Selby and Wensley, 1990:10-11).

Some change is inevitable since the adaptation moves from one art form to another. The case studies also move from one form to another.

The primary text was the research data. This has been adapted into a performance, though the degree of change has caused anxiety for the researchers.

> Even the most well-intentioned, indeed slavish adapter will have to adapt (change) a book, or short story, and perhaps even a play; certainly in regard to a novel, the possibility of altering nothing can be dismissed. Disagreement comes only when we discuss the nature and degree of such alteration as will take place, for some modes of alteration will seem 'faithful' to a given book, and others will seem a 'betrayal'. (Beja, 1979:81).

As Beja adds, 'Betrayal is a strong word' (*ibid*). But this betrayal is often felt by those who know the source text and feel the adaptation does not comply with their imaginations. A struggle with the risk of betrayal is precisely what we find in the case studies. Wagner sees some adaptations as 'violations' (1975:222), an emotive term which also expresses the anxiety for the ethnodramatist.

Inevitably there has been discussion and disagreement about adaptations and the degree to which new versions have wandered from the authenticity of the source text and some are even considered to have been sacrilegious in their departures, particularly films adapted from classic texts. However, there is also a view that a different genre requires different treatment and so you would not expect that the source text could be entirely reproduced into a secondary text of a different genre. There are differences in what can be achieved in different genres and responses to adaptations are often personal. Some see changes in the genre as compromising the faithfulness to the original but some do not. Jill simply considered moving from one written genre to another, from research report into dialogue. She found that this genre adaptation made something new possible, as members of the group described the way in which the embodied data in the script forced an identification with the characters which data extracts in reports were less likely to do. Moving from written recorded data to full performance offers many other opportunities, as both Linden and Alice vividly illustrate.

The similarities are obvious. We can conceive of research data as the source text and the performances as the secondary text. The same questions of faithfulness apply and adaptation theory may usefully be applied to ethnodrama to aid critical analysis of what is taking place.

What might distinguish the activities is the degree to which 'it matters' and therefore the degree of responsibility the adapter feels to the source. When the material is people and their stories, rather than say, a classic novel, it is less easy to shrug off the differences created by moving from one source to the other. The responsibility on the shoulders of the ethnodramatist is significant. Interestingly, Jill found that, albeit irrationally, she felt more responsibility to the participants and their stories when she was adapting the research findings into a scripted piece than when she adapted them into a regular research report. This is interesting since the participants and their stories were exactly the same.

Performance as reality or fiction

Jill explains that even having constructed the script almost entirely from verbatim data, it was still 'a creative act to put together the words of participants in the form that I chose.' But she asks, 'can fiction be said to represent reality of experience?' She refers to the problem of the 'tensions between what is real and what is fictional in a script'.

Linden grapples with these issues in relation to live performance and the pretend, noting that if one can accept that performance is by nature artificial, one can perhaps allow for degrees of authenticity. Performance creates fictions to depict reality and Kate considers how she would like to achieve this for the Scrap Pickers drama. She would have liked smells and additional sounds to build the context in which the scrap pickers work. Her desire to give the audience a real sense of what life is like for these disadvantaged elderly people seems to take priority. She would have liked the smell of rotting vegetables, wet cardboard and traffic fumes to have enhanced the audience's experience even further, though, as she acknowledges, probably not their enjoyment. So such effects would be real in the sense of being real smells and sounds, but unreal in the sense that they would be created artificially in a studio. Linden might conceive this as a degree of authenticity, as she states that fabrication is an integral component of performance. The pretend helps to create the authenticity of the lives of the scrap pickers.

Alice does not attempt to depict real life. Non-realistic presentation style and the part of a researcher commenting on the action keep the audience well aware of that. Exaggeration is included and it makes the audience laugh. But the non-realistic moments, such as the exaggeration, give us recognition of real life experiences. Being set on a university campus and the audiences having been employed in or associated with higher education, there are glimpses of the familiar which evoke wider recognition in our own lives. *Alice Hoy is Not a Building* is also real life in the sense that it presents the shared thoughts and encounters of the four researcher actors. The researcher role expresses the process the four have been through. Ethnodramatists have the task of presenting real stories in performance in whichever way they feel will best tell their stories. Not being life-like may be the most effective way to depict life.

The interest and emotion of viewers of television programmes and films are often heightened if they are watching something based on real life. Recognition of artistic license is sometimes forgotten in the focus on the real people in a real dilemma. Equally, the realness of ethnodrama evokes additional interest. This is the case even though the script is a blend of the real, as in the actual words spoken, and fiction, as in words added by the ethnodramatist in order to maintain confidentiality or help depict a context or deliver the project aims. This question of the relationship between reality and fiction is examined in detail in the next chapter.

The gatekeepers and power

Mienczakowski proposes that 'unlike other academic reporting processes, it [ethnodrama] leaves conclusions to the discretion of its audiences' (1994). But this seems to deny the implications of choices made at every level by the ethnodramatist, the actors and the directors. An audience's conclusions are shaped by the performance, which is a construction by the individual ethnodramatist, the production team or both. So the conclusions left to the audience's discretion are only possible because of the ethnodramatist's construction. There is no neutral display of options for the audience. Linden neatly concludes that all decisions involve the playwright's bias. The ethnographers of the nineteenth century are criticised for taking their colonial attitudes into their observations of researched communities. They reported on the 'other' and made meaning out of what they saw by relating it to their own experiences. Now that we are more sceptical of the grand narratives, the researcher is conscious of the risk of colonising research participant communities. We acknowledge research 'participants' rather than referring to the 'researched'. However, there still lurks the positioned glance, even after the demise of the innocent eye. It is this affected, blurred gaze that informs the ethnodrama journey. No matter how we try, we cannot be completely objective. The ethnodramatist chooses which are the privileged and which are the silenced voices and as Alexander simply expresses it, 'who gets to speak and for whom' (2005: 11). Madison is emphatic, telling her readers, 'You have the power to tell their story and to have the last word on how they will be represented'. (2005:33.)

This leaves the ethnodramatist with a lot of control. It is not only power in the presentation but power in the research process too. Decisions are made at every stage of the research and performance process. Let us consider the journey from a research participant's initial recorded conversation with a researcher, using as an example the British black police officer interviews which were presented in a DVD that was used for police equality and diversity awareness training (Ackroyd and Pilkington, 2008 conference paper). The DVD depicts a fictional group of police officers at an equality and diversity training workshop which includes the showing of three (real) monologues of black police officers relating their experiences. The journey of the initial transcripts charts the competing interests of stakeholders and the tensions of different demands these are considered further in the next chapter..

Before the oral histories were recorded the experiences of individuals had already been subject to processes of narrative construction and reconstruction, since experiences are always interpreted and in this sense constructed. The construction becomes more obvious with the advent of oral histories. The following stages can be distinguished:

1. The narrative is given in a tape-recorded interview to a researcher who is interested in the experiences of minority groups in the police. Here a range of factors comes into play and influences the narrative: the relation between the interviewer and interviewee, the location of the interview, the questions asked, the assumed purpose of the question, the power dynamics involved and the identities of those involved.

2. The transcription, not always accurate, of the interview is produced by somebody who was not necessarily present at the interview. This subtracts from the interview non-verbal cues such as gestures, facial expressions and tone of voice etc. The actual words are only a small part of the communication. While these omissions may be put back later by an actor, the non-verbal cues are by no means necessarily the same.

3. The selection is done by a white producer, himself not a police officer but a sociologist, of which transcripts might be used in the DVD. Eleven transcribed interviews are available from which to choose. Factors influencing which transcripts to forward to the scriptwriter, who is experienced in ethnodrama, include judgements about the clarity of the narrative, whether it incorporates issues such as stop and search that might be addressed in the training, and whether it grabs attention and is perceived by the sociologist as 'dramatically exciting'. In this way selection of what is sent to the scriptwriter already assumes a sense of what might be interesting as well as what might serve the purpose of training. These aesthetic considerations are explored in depth in Chapter 5.

4. The scriptwriter incorporates selected parts of selected transcripts into the script. He selects three of the five that have been forwarded to him and then chooses the sections he thinks will work artistically. They are too long as they are, but he wants to keep them 'as raw as possible' – in other words without interference. The testimonies are now located in particular spaces in the script of the DVD and thus heard between the dialogue of the fictional characters. The way they are placed in the script also affects how they are perceived. What comes before and after, shapes how an action or scene is seen.

5. The testimonies are changed by the scriptwriter because the producer and ethnodramatist project partner decide that they are not as clear as they need to be. A tendency to go off at tangents means that the selected transcripts are too convoluted for the key points to be communicated. 'Erhs' and repetitions of real speech don't seem right in the film script.

6. At a read through with the actors, the testimonies are considered to be far too long. The cameraman and film editor claims that he is 'losing the will to live' in relation to one of the testimonies, and everyone except the producer and scriptwriter feel that they are somewhat tedious. At the reading the testimonies originally conveyed orally by individuals in their own words are now spoken by other people. If the director, cameraman/editor and actors had their way, the testimonies would be cut to snippets. A division opens up here between artistry and instrumentality, between aesthetic considerations and the need for the original stories to be appropriately honoured.

7. The scriptwriter asks to shorten the whole script and particularly to cut the testimonials. Thus he is now cutting a hybrid of the original words (those the sociologist had selected) and his own. The testimonies still remain longer than the director and actors like but the producer and scriptwriter are reluctant to jettison what the producer and scriptwriter feel are real and moving stories central to the film. They are concerned to retain those stories as they incorporate issues that can be taken up later in the training.

8. There is a reading and performance of the scripted testimonials by the actors auditioned and those selected. Do they read the whole script? Do they understand the context of what they are doing? Little about the professional actors' performances feels real or lived. Indeed in some places the words are not delivered as they have been written. So here is another new 'text'.

And the stages do not end there. The two of us view the final DVD with the overall purpose of the project in mind. We consider that the testimonies are crucial to the telling of the real stories and for grabbing the attention of the workshop participants, just as Jill described from her case study. For while the rest of the script is fun, here the participants need to be shocked into the reality of these people's experiences. We do not think the testimonies as they stand achieve that. A decision is therefore made to cut and re-film the testimonies in the DVD with different actors. So the journey of the officers' stories continues.

Breaking the stages up in this way demonstrates the significant number of moves from the participants' original words. While many ethnodramatists will not be including film, this process is clearly the same.

Other influences of power

Linden appears to move into a different gear when the company of professionals took over her script. Her recognition that the play had another community to serve refers to the company who had a show to put on. The ethnodramatist is not the only powerful influence on the journey between a participant's story and the audience experience. There are the players in between and the decisions they make regarding the communication processes.

Relationships between researcher and participant

There is often a problem in the power dynamics between the researcher and the research participants, especially if the participants perceive themselves as less empowered and carry less cultural capital. The Hong Kong students were anxious about speaking to the scrap pickers in case the elderly people working on the street felt frightened or scared of the educated research students. Patti Lather surprised many when she spoke of talking to research participants in the hot tub (2001, IDIERI Ohio, keynote address). Her aim is to ensure that the participants feel comfortable and to endeavour to address the cultural and social power differentials between researcher and participant. Participants in a hot tub, or similar place where they feel comfortable, may relax and be able to speak more easily. One may ponder the balance between ensuring that participants are relaxed to speak, and ensuring that they are in a position where they are most likely to speak freely. There may be an implication that they may be inclined to speak more freely than they may have intended. Either way, Lather has fore-grounded the need to work against a hierarchy between researcher and research participant so that the participant may feel more of a co-researcher. Underlying her work is a deep desire for researchers to respect the participants and pay attention to their stories.

These are concerns for all qualitative researchers but what is crucial for us is the move of participants' stories into performance and the relative power to affect what emerges. In Hong Kong the students worried that if they explained to the scrap pickers what their stories would be used for, the pickers might not wish to get involved. Kate raises an interesting point about experience and confidence in relation to both the participants' and students' experiences:

> Once interviews were completed, there was no further contact with informants, thereby denying them the opportunity to control text or representation. Even if we had chosen a more articulate and confident group, our own inexperience would have made us fearful of allowing them the kind of involvement suggested. We felt barely in control of presenting the data ourselves, to have allowed an element of control by the subjects was beyond our capabilities at that time.

Richard painstakingly discussed every step in his project with both the teachers and the students in the participant drama class. Sometimes this led him to feel torn by what he saw as the appropriate way forward and what they thought. Regarding the students' suggestion to use their real names, he asked himself whether he had to abandon another of the ethical principles which he had established for his project, and respond to the wishes of his student participants, even if he had misgivings. Interestingly, he discussed the issue with the teachers and together they agreed to use pseudonyms. With the best and most open attitude, it is still the ethnodramatist who holds the responsibility and makes decisions and must do so.

Researcher's voice

The inclusion of a researcher in performance created a struggle for both Jill and Alice for different reasons. Jill's angst was about power and control. She continues to be concerned about her decision to include a researcher's voice in her script because she is suspicious of its controlling power: she wondered whether she was not allowing the data from the participants to speak for itself, whether she was not trusting the reader or audience to come to the right conclusions, and whether she could not resist the opportunity to lead the audience to find what she had from the data and instead was inserting her own rhetoric to exert control. On the other hand, she also felt that there would be something dishonest about not exposing the researcher and her explicit role. She questioned whether if there had there been no researcher role in the script she would have been guilty of obscuring the co-constructed nature of the data and her authorship. She saw her dilemma as in a way similar to that of scientists writing of their work in the third person to create an illusion of objectivity.

Saldaña suggests that ethnodramatists must ask, 'whose story is it?' (1998) in an attempt to take ethnodramatists back to their participants. There is clearly a moral imperative to respect the stories given. But let's not deceive ourselves that we won't diminish the story that is racist or chauvinist or at least present it in such a way that the audience does not leave assuming that the ethnodramatist holds that view. All stories are equal but some are more equal than others. It is ultimately the ethno-dramatist who is the gatekeeper, determining which stories will be presented and how, no matter the extent to which the process is shared, as we saw in Richard's project. This is a great responsibility. Ideally, the process 'involves ... ways of using performance as a means, method, and mode of communication establishing an intercultural dialogue' (Alexander, 2005:415). In conceiving the work as an opportunity for intercultural dialogue we must accept that choices will be made on the way. Whatever those choices are the ethnodramatist must be ready, as we have seen, to 'be accountable for the consequences of our repre-sentations and the implications of our messages – because they matter.' (Madison, 2005:5)

5

AESTHETIC AND OTHER TENSIONS

By the time the truth has become a play, it's already a fabrication.
(Linden Chapter 8)

This is the arresting conclusion of our contributor Linden, paraphrasing Paul Brown, the author of *Aftershocks* (1993), one of Australia's most celebrated and often performed pieces of that close cousin of ethnodrama, verbatim theatre, entirely based on the words of survivors of Newcastle's 1989 earthquake disaster. It's a statement which make any ethnographic researcher with integrity nervous and it highlights the key tensions to be dealt with in this chapter: the problematic, enticing and complex relationship between the needs and demands of recording and representing the life of a community to somebody and those of making a play.

Johnny Saldaña takes a bold position on the business of making a play, which puts some other agendas we have seen creeping in, such as education and therapy, firmly in their place:

> Theatre's primary goal is neither to educate nor enlighten. Theatre's primary goal is to entertain – to *entertain ideas as it entertains its spectators* ... an entertainingly informative experience for an audience, one that is aesthetically sound, intellectually rich and emotionally evocative (2005:14).

He advises his students accordingly: 'stop thinking like a social scientist and start thinking like an artist' (p33). This appears at first sight to put researchers in our place too but Saldaña recognises that the relationship is no such simple dichotomy, but rather that there are a range of truths in representation, and moreover that 'the best lens for fieldwork views human action dramatistically' (*ibid*).

Our case study writers recognise this too. Wrestling with the relationship, they come up with a diverse range of attitudes and starting points. Richard took the cautious position that he would avoid including material that was dramatically engaging yet uncharacteristic of what usually took place and also that any dialogue constructed for the ethnographic performance would be quoted verbatim from what was recorded in the field, either from observation or interview. The words and actions of the participants would not be imaginatively re-worked to the extent that they were unrecognisable from the context in which they originated. Alice were more excited by the aesthetic possibilities than they were deterred by fears of misrepresentation; they were representing themselves, so they had no problems with member-checking. They had no qualms in using a range of performance techniques including improvisation, character development, role-play, symbolism, manipulation of dramatic elements, scriptwriting and rehearsal processes to explore and transform verbatim data. In fact, they went much further and used drama processes not only as a way to communicate their research but also as 'essentially an act of discovery'.

Richard, working to his carefully negotiated responsibilities with a group of students in an institutional setting, was often troubled when confronted with an incident in a class or told something by one of his participants which caught his interest as a dramatist. At such times, because it could potentially misrepresent what he had typically observed, he decided to include the material only if it could be crystallised by other incidents and opinions. However, even he was willing to 'cut myself a bit of slack' by providing some scope within the writing processes for artistic freedom and the expression of imaginative possibilities.

The literature and our contributors agree that verisimilitude and re-creation of a community with integrity do not just reside in mimetic representation. There are multiple truths which can be both shared and artistically satisfying, even in the most potentially sensitive and fraught areas of content. Gray *et al* (2000), devising ethnodrama on living with cancer, note:

Whilst we felt it was important to stay closely connected to the research base of the studies, we collectively agreed to numerous explorations beyond word-for-word excerpts from transcripts. Some of these departures were simply to allow for clearer expression of thoughts that study participants had articulated. Other explorations were more related to artistic considerations, and the desire to produce a compelling presentation that would entertain and engage an audience, not just inform them. All (100%) of those attending presentations for the public agreed or strongly agreed that they enjoyed the drama, and that they benefited from seeing it. Similarly, 99 per cent agreed or strongly agreed that there 'was a lot of truth in this drama'. (p140)

Jill expresses her disappointment that she had not been bolder in her first venture with participants facing serious health crises and believes that far from compromising the integrity of the research, further dramatisation would have enhanced it. In the light of her experience she would not be so fearful next time of fictionalising more of the script, particularly where verbatim data in itself could not adequately portray an important interpretation of the data: she would also pay more attention to the credibility of all the characters. She believes that developing a fictitious back-story for the researcher would have been more believable in the script and so have demonstrated the co-constructed nature of the data more effectively.

The elements of aesthetic form: dialogue and fiction

Like Richard, Jill puts her finger on the important decision which has to be made about whether or not to fictionalise the dialogue and the limitations caused by their reluctance to do so. Of course any verbal testimony or record of behaviour can be translated into good dramatic dialogue but only by selection and transformation which inevitably means taking a step away from an authentic rendition of the original. This problem was faced and partially acknowledged by Jim Mienczakowski and his colleagues in their ethnodramas about health when they decided to alter the words of the witnesses only to a minimum in terms of aesthetic shaping (Mienczakowski, 1994:47; they also had informal discussions with the co-author of this book at the performances 1993, 1994). This was in part to properly honour the voices of the witnesses, such as people with mental illness. The research team had a further agenda: they hoped that the play would have a psychotherapeutic effect on the witnesses, who would be among the audience at one of the performances. One of the authors of this book watched the piece but was not in a position to evaluate the success of the piece as psychotherapy. However, in John's view, that very worthy decision not to tamper with the witnesses' words had two inevitable corollaries for other audiences: one aesthetic and one educational. First, the actors, who were themselves nursing and drama students with limited performing skills, were provided with dialogue that was often undramatic and pedestrian. Second, this dialogue was beyond the students' capability to turn into powerful theatre and the performance was largely unshaped dramaturgically as a piece of informative, in other words educational, theatre for audiences of other school and tertiary students. It was therefore a less than electrifying theatrical experience, and came over as explicit and didactic. Wherever we turn in this genre, we are faced with swings and roundabouts.

Interestingly, the full-time professional theatre worker and playwright among our contributors, Linden, chose to anchor her work on the faithful reproduction of testimony given by her witnesses (after all, she calls it verbatim theatre). Only once, she confesses, she switched a piece of given text, itself not altered, for structural convenience from the mouth of one character to that of another, who was serving a similar function in the play. She was then faced with a problem common to many a playwright when the director of her final version encouraged the actors to *ad lib...* It was problematic for her because of her commitment to stick to verbatim script, which paradoxically the actors found important. Of all the others, even the cautious Richard decided upon a strategy whereby he amalgamated the words and actions of more than one student to form composite characters, while Jill invented fictitious dialogue to put over some of the data and wished that her inexperience and fear had not led her to 'slavishly adhere to the sometimes-faltering utterances of the verbatim data'.

Elements of aesthetic form: *mise-en-scène*

The dialogue and language is only part of the dramatic transformation which data gathered from a community goes through to become performance. Virtually all the other elements of dramatic form go through the mincer too. First of all the location is almost invariably changed, except on the rare occasions when the piece is performed on site, like the

Norwegian football fan-club. Usually, however, a *mise-en-scène* has to be created, either physically, or in the case of Reader's Theatre, in the audience's head. At the most physical extreme is the meticulous and laborious work of ethnographers such as Joni L. Jones. She invited her audience to wander through and experience *in toto* a carefully constructed Yoruba market, as authentically re-created as possible with the smells, sounds and action of the real thing: tastes, smells, cooking, things to touch and do, drumming and dancing and singing and actors ready to explain what they were doing, or would have been in the real location. She then deliberately and cleverly disrupted this 'faithful' representation – 'my way to complicate authenticity' – to problematise the whole question of the exotic, and presumably to challenge the audience's perception of the 'other' nature of the community represented by the colour-blind casting of a white woman to play the role of Jones herself, who is a black Yoruba woman. She acknowledges that this confused some of the audience considerably (Jones, 2002:1-15).

On a much smaller scale and limited budget, our Hong Kong Scrap Pickers took on-stage verisimilitude seriously too. They wanted to give their audience, as much as possible 'not a sense of 'being there', but during performance 'being here'', as Saldaña puts it (2005:141). Their brief research had given them a strong kinaesthetic sense of the physical reality of their informant group experience and they felt that their own experience as performing artists gave them sufficient techniques to reproduce that reality to some degree, through the blocking and careful reproduction of movement and physical restrictions and extensive use of appropriate costumes and props.

Linden, who did have access to a theatre, chose to represent the scene of the event that she was re-creating – which was a train crash that scarred its whole community – with a realism that was well-distanced: she employed photographs and film of the crash scene. These were not horrific close-ups but fragments of scenes distanced by irony: routine shots of the line, graffiti, peaceful corners, and retrospectively significant railway notices. Alice also chose not to represent some historical scenes and memories physically but to depict the invisible women of the past in another location entirely as disembodied voices that the central characters hear when they find themselves in the basement of their building, which was represented physically in a stylised way. This setting within a setting and the characters' ambiguous responses to the voices evoked multiple meanings 'in the space between action and audience'.

Fictionalisation and authenticity

Paul Brown reminds us that all drama is a fiction, even verbatim theatre, where every word of the dialogue is provided by the participants: 'Aftershocks is a fabrication, just like any drama spun from a writer's head' (1993:i). Creating a *mise-en-scène* is another step into make-believe for all except those site-specific ethnodramas such as the Norwegian soccer fan-clubbers playing away on location. However, fictionalisation is not the same as a retreat from authenticity. It can enhance the truthfulness of the research as well as the experience of the audiences. Jill makes this startling discovery for herself, that in presenting data as fictitious dialogue she was able to portray triangulation between participant groups in ways that were not available to her in writing a standard research report. The live juxtapositions of different voices can reveal and emphasise important data analysis links and themes.

Victor and Jumai are bold in their trust in the value of fictionalisation: fictionalising witnesses' narratives and voices 'places the project in a different orbit', encouraging their audience to engage with the performance and creating a continuing critical dialogue between the audience and what they are watching. However, they were forced to wrestle with the tensions between the biographical and the fictional, which raised questions of authenticity (is this story still true?), ownership (is it still mine?) and power (do I still have a say in and control over my story?). They then decided that the script itself would be inspired by the source materials but not limited to it. As a draft working script it would be subject to deconstruction and reconstruction by the team, by participants at open readings, workshops and rehearsals and subsequently by the performers during the rehearsal process. The aim was to maintain dialogue with the material and to integrate moments of creative action with moments of creative reflection.

Other dramatic elements

In order to map better the complex landscape of meaning lying between the words fiction and authenticity, we must examine what we and our contributors mean by fictionalisation. They are talking about a number of mostly distinct, if overlapping, transformative processes which take place between the data collection and what the audience (whichever audience) is presented with. They are talking about transforming the words of the witnesses themselves into coherent and dramatically acceptable dialogue. Inevitably they are talking about transforming the space and its ambience – the whole performance context – in which the dramatic encounter between the original community and the audience happens.

They are also concerned about structural issues: the re-shaping of data into new and effectively fictional configurations, especially of time and narrative. Victor and Jumai worry about appropriating the witnesses' stories. Linden worries on the macro and micro level. On the macro level she is aware that she had a three-way responsibility: to the research, to the witnesses, and to the play. In her five-scene structure she found herself organising the content according to the key themes that emerged in the research. For the witnesses this might not have provided an adequate platform for their contributions, nor have been theatrically the most arresting or engaging form to present the material. She agonised over the lack of a climax and dénouement, but recognised that this would not have been true either to the themes of the research or the experiences of the participants. At micro level, her playwright's instincts told her that intercutting scenes and snippets from different occasions adds a necessary dramatic energy charge but takes away from immediate authenticity.

Stylisation

Intercutting dialogue and action in order to generate economy and pace is one of the simplest manifestations of stylisation. That implies the distancing and shaping into something else of verbatim and action data which, as a feature and requirement of the research methodology called ethnography, has been collected as naturalistically as possible. The most obvious convention to use for transmitting this data as simply as possible would appear to be naturalism, but fortunately, few ethnographic dramatists have chosen this path, just as few creators of dramatic performance and dramatists down the centuries have. As any playwright or student of literature knows, the convention of stage naturalism, which first emerged around the beginning of the twentieth century (just in time for movies and television), is a complex artifice and highly stylised. It is dependent on embedded cues to mask the artificiality and create the illusion of real life, as well as an extreme manipulation of the performance space, light and sound. This happens through the deprivation of any other sensory cues from the real environment that might distract the audience, and replacing them by unreal 'realistic' performance space, design, light and sound, intensely fabricated dialogue, deep and 'rounded' characterisation and 'lifelike' acting with real emotion and tears as required. This sophistication has all been largely beyond the usually limited spaces and resources available to ethnodramatists. Saldaña puts it succinctly as far as the performance space is concerned:

> From my own experience I offer the classic design adage for guidance: 'Less is more'. A projected slide of Brad's cabin in Harry's woodlands is easier to create than rebuilding the actual cabin to scale and mounting it onstage. (2005:28)

This would certainly have a much more authentic ring to the audience. Those professionals in ethnodrama and kindred areas who have had access to such sophistication, such as Kaufman and his teams on Broadway in *The Laramie Project* and *I Am My Own Wife*, or Paul Brown himself in *Aftershocks*, didn't go anywhere near naturalism. For many audience members of *Laramie* there was an interesting and unresolved tension between the sparse minimalism of the set and understated acting style and the theatre which had been built primarily for naturalism and theatre of illusion, and this tension added an extra dimension to the emotional power of that play. Nor did they try to recreate naturalistically any of the violence of either the acts or the attitudes which formed the basis of the story and the company's investigation. Linden, who was offered a well-equipped theatre, chose Johnny Saldaña's solution and projected photographs and film of the original location, not lurid ones, to create her *mise-en-scène* and bring the audience just close enough to, just far enough away from, her fatal subject matter.

Reader's Theatre

Many a sophisticated ethnographer/dramaturge and many a neophyte who is dabbling in reporting through performance for the first time have found a much more reasonable starting point in Reader's Theatre. As Donmoyer and Yennie-Donmoyer assert: 'in Reader's Theatre stylization and certain conventions are used for the express purpose of de-emphasising realism ... realism is also minimized by the use of stylization' (1998:398-399). This convention, where a text comprising selected extracts from the research data, arranged dialogically, is simply read by performers, seems to offer a fairly uncomplicated and direct path from the witnesses' words to the audience's consciousness without the addition of aesthetic transformation. Some of the enthusiastic reports of research practitioners coming to ethnodrama for the first time bear testimony to this, like this account from the field of children's nursing:

> The listener can experience parents' decisions; changes in attitude, surprise, self-appraisal, directness and love for their children... the parents voices are clearly represented. Many who have heard this text have reported that they had not previously understood the complexities. The intimacy of parents' conversations moves us and encourages us to know more. These are the hoped-for outcomes when a text is performed. (Smith and Gallo 2007:526)

However, it can only take you so far, especially when the material being presented is not so immediately empathy-ripe as the above to ring sentimental bells for the audience. There have been not a few dull and pedestrian attempts to present, as ethnographic performance, text read live or read and minimally moved by embodied actors, which have perished from their own worthiness. In all of these that we have come across, some of which were by experienced practitioners who ought to have known better, the performers were unable or unwilling to start where the audience is at, which is wanting to be entertained, as Saldaña reminds us, and take enough aesthetic steps to transform the data into something engaging. Our contributor Jill, a fledgling exponent, quickly recognised the limitations of her cautious approach to the use of data. By initially choosing extracts of data which best exemplified the findings taken from the fully indexed data archive, she felt she had failed to produce anything that came close to credible dialogue or a coherent script. So she took steps to remedy this. Even so she rued her lack of adventurousness in not being sufficiently willing to depart from the verbatim transcripts, and used the Donmoyers' theory to acknowledge that the use of stylisation in the staging encourages the audience member to actively construct meaning and engage with the issues presented. In fact, as the Donmoyers point out, even Reader's Theatre is a highly stylised activity where actors behave quite unlike those in naturalistic theatre (1998:398-400).

This sparse stylisation is not without its pitfalls. In an account of a slightly augmented piece of Reader's Theatre that is admirable for its willingness to re-evaluate and then re-engage with the form, Sheryl Cozart and her colleagues re-live their contrasting experiences of performing the same piece to two different sets of hearers. Their first appreciative audience for their ethnodrama on research into a new teachers' programme was comprised of fellow researchers at a national conference. Emboldened, they performed it to some of those teachers.

> What was intended to give voice to a polyphony of perspectives and present data in a theoretically playful manner became problematic in front of this audience. While we intended to engage the audience in playing along with our metaphor of performance, instead we encountered resistance to our themes, challenges to our accuracy and suspicions about our motives. (Cozart *et al*, 2003:54)

With courage and perspicacity, they identified the problem as a mono-logic approach which failed to address the need of an audience of the community of their original witnesses to have their voice and their say and appeared to them to be patronising them by its distant and ironic playfulness. Possibly also neither the research team's performance, nor the performance convention of Reader's Theatre/ethnodrama, were strong enough to convey their intended playfulness with sufficient charm to beguile this critical second audience. From their experience, Cozart and colleagues constructed a much more robust set of principles which might well be followed by intending ethnodramatists.

Our contributor Linden had to reconsider her position in a discomfort-ing version of the same context-specific negative response. An audience member who turned out to be a relative of one of the victims of the rail crash accused her of sensationalism in one scene, of failing to provide warning of the play's emotional potential and of failing to debrief the audience. As she recounts, she addressed the second and third accusa-tions, but on thorough reflection maintained that the 'sensational' scene was not sensational and kept it unchanged.

Cozart *et al* also incidentally put their finger on a crucial element in the whole question of stylisation, when they talk about their 'metaphor of performance', a metaphor which was not understood or accepted by the audience, so became part of the problem. But in one sense theatrical stylisation is itself a form of embodied metaphor, as becomes clear in this account by medical researchers of their simple effort to integrate theatrical form and original data, which was successful, judging by the evaluations they quote:

> Whilst we felt it was important to stay closely connected to the research base of the studies, we collectively agreed to numerous explorations beyond word-for-word excerpts from transcripts. Some of these departures... were related to artistic considerations, and the desire to produce a compelling presentation that would entertain and engage an audience. For example in one scene various well-meaning and not-so-well-meaning friends push a woman with metastatic breast cancer back and forth from one side of the stage to the other, all the while giving unsolicited advice. This image represents what we heard from women, but is not of course literally what happened to them. (Gray *et al*, 2000:140)

The authors go on to deduce from the 'many comments about the image's usefulness for portraying the emotional situation of ill women' that 'seeing women pushed around provided a more direct pathway to the lived 'truth' of their experiences than a compilation of verbal statements ever could have' (*ibid*).

Dramatic structure

Style or stylisation and dramatic structure are indivisible. Saldaña (2003:221) provocatively gives us a temptingly glib definition of an ethnodrama as 'a data corpus with all the boring parts taken out'. Our Hong Kong contributors wrestled hard and perceptively with problems of dramatic structure. Quite properly as researchers, Will and Terrence went back to that data corpus and its demands, constraints and possibilities, noting that Saldaña's dictum may sometimes be difficult to fulfil because as researchers they neither could nor should omit important but less interesting or digestible data from their research participants. Luckily for both of them they found that in their two projects most important pieces of data carried surprises and dramatic impacts. Terrence focused objectively on the case data. Most of the pieces of selected data were interesting in themselves and naturally provided mini-episodes that echoed or contrasted with each other. He did not need to try to twist them into a narrative with a linear development, nor to assume anything other than a realistic style: for him an abstract style would lead to interpretation by the audience involving value judgments.

Will acutely started by interrogating the data through his version of Dorothy Heathcote's '5 Ws' of process drama structure: What['s happening]? When? Where? Who to? and What's at stake?. He decided that his team must sequence their data properly according to those principles and 'invent some lighter scenes in between the meaningful but heavier scenes'. Will also mentions an interesting concomitant: that if an ethno-drama had an underlying educational purpose – in other words one of those non-ethnographic agendas, as theirs did – this actually helped the performance find a focus or structure. His colleague Kate points out that they deliberately didn't make full use of the range of theatrical tools available to them and confirms that movement was literal, not symbolic and that they chose literal modes of expression. Their rationale for this was that for their intended audience of school students the issue itself was 'heavy' enough, without the addition of layers of complex theatrical coding or symbolism that might alienate them. However, in retrospect, she regrets the missed possibilities of a more symbolic approach, both in terms of the words and particularly of the physicality.

Alice, although they remained concerned that their reach for a strongly dramatic process might overwhelm or distort the methodological integrity of their ethnographic research practice, nevertheless dived boldly into symbolic and stylised playwriting and performance techniques: including improvisation, character development, role play, symbolism, manipulation of dramatic elements, scriptwriting and rehearsal processes to explore and transform verbatim data. They consciously addressed the elements of dramatic form, such as space, contrast, conflict, climax, timing, tension, mood, rhythm, sound, symbol, focus and language. They discovered, as Gray et al (2000) had discovered, that layers of meaning in the data could be revealed through theatrical artifice, such as parallel storytelling, moments of stillness and comic timing and more distanced techniques still, like clowning and even magic realism. Where the voices from the data are framed in a complex fantasy scene, multiple meanings emerge for the audience both from the voices and the responses of the lightly fictionalised characters.

Characters and acting

Which brings us to the questions of character and characterisation. Just how much liberty can researchers take with the people whom they are supposed to be representing? Can they create fictional characters? Should they simplify the characterisation to the depiction of characteristics which they have observed or inferred from their data or can they complicate the characters to make them lifelike? At one end of the spectrum of ethnography – the Reader's Theatre end – and in a lot of verbatim theatre, the performers just read the voices of the community or enact their actions quite neutrally, foregrounding the words and actions themselves, and trusting that they will make their own effect and meaning. They do not invent or create composite characters. The first public reading of *Aftershocks* was effectively an ethnodrama, where the playwright/researcher eloquently sums up this minimalist position, which he notes is typical of most verbatim theatre in Britain, too.

> The performance was given by eight members of the research team, who read from loose-leaf folders. Staging was extremely simple, with basic blocking [but there was blocking!] no costumes or props. Each reader played two or three different real life characters – including the people they themselves had interviewed – but with no attempt to exactly mimic the real person's physical or linguistic mannerisms, other than what the words on the page dictated [but those *were* imitated!]. As far as 'acting' goes, the readers simply attempted to tell stories to the audience. (Brown, 1993:xiv, xvi)

The choice, editing and arrangement of the data have inevitably turned the dialogue and performance into a transformation of the data.

Our contributors came from several different starting points and made different decisions. Though, like other verbatim theatre creators, Linden chose to stick with her original witnesses, and not invent any characters, she did come up against a couple of major problems for a dramatist, especially in telling the story in something like a chronological sequence and trying to make the characters seem real. She was initially stumped by discovering that contrary to her expectations, the data did not fit with the conventional three-act play. There were no entrapments, no dénouement and, worst of all, no Hero, nor characters out of whose actions she could fashion heroism, which she later cleverly identifies elsewhere. For the participants there wasn't necessarily any development of character nor emotions, which are a mainstay of dramatic narrative and tension. She did eventually manage to find a little, but to keep the audience interested in those characters she had to find other ways, theatrical ways. Here she departed from classic practice and gave her actors the right to evoke nuances in the text which may not have been in the original transcript. They found verisimilitude through the powerful actor's and director's tools of silence and body position, for example, and for a physicalisation of the text through movement on stage which was not present in the original interviews which were themselves the rather odd artifice that is typical of ethnographical research of textual narratives collected by a researcher *in situ* with the speakers seated, entirely disconnected from each other. Like all our contributors, she also looked to metaphor to animate the text.

Near the same end of the spectrum, Jill and Richard both took one important step towards characterisation: the creation of composite characters, who could economically present complex perspectives and viewpoints from the data. Jill candidly admits that the characters as she represented them were not to be found amongst the research participants, nor were the off-stage people they referred to in their dialogue. This individual liberty was however specifically designed to convey some broader truths about the shared experiences of the witnesses. Richard tried this too, partly to shelter individual witnesses from dialogue which could easily identify them. He got some unexpected feedback from the students who were strongly ambivalent about this: they realised that individual identities could be worked out within the composite characters from tell-tale lines and rather resented his diplomacy in concealing them in this way. The students, rather than being resentful or defensive, were fascinated by the thought that an actor portraying them in the play might make judgements about the person behind the character. In response, Richard decided to dispense with the practice of constructing the protagonists from multiple students who exhibited similar characteristics. Instead, each of the main student characters in the play would be based on a particular student in the respective classes. However, to ensure that as wide a range of viewpoints as possible was represented in the play, he would still create some subsidiary composite characters who would be referred to by the nomenclature of Boy or Girl.

The inexperience of the Hong Kong students and the need for caution because their ethnodramas were being assessed, plus their own sense of probity, made them nervous at first of taking any liberties with their informants' texts in terms of characterisation. But many of them were spurred by other constraints or considerations into inviting the audiences to take imaginative leaps. For Elayne and her colleagues the constraint of time to research their witnesses' backgrounds meant they had to give themselves some 'artistic licence' to imagine what an Indonesian maid's husband was like, or their life back in her village in Indonesia. To do this, they turned like Alice to the power of metaphor and to the use of powerful physical symbols such as rice – or rather lack of it – to show poverty and a sarong to represent things close to the maid, items which they had to guess would be important to her. The scrap pickers were bolder still, and invented a couple of entirely fictional characters, two 'old geezers' who were deliberate stereotypes and both comic and ironic, so they could convey certain information they needed the audience to know.

Victor and Jumai were inevitably concerned about how they represented their witnesses from the point of view of authenticity, ownership and power, because they acknowledged from the start they would be working with both biographical and fictional materials. Spin-offs from this entailed both ethical and copyright considerations. As a draft working script it would be subject to deconstruction and reconstruction by the team, by participants at open readings, workshops and rehearsals and by the performers during the rehearsal process. Their aim was to maintain dialogue with the material and to integrate moments of creative action with moments of creative reflection. They realised that this challenged two notions: of the script as sacrosanct and of sole authorship. They feel the result is a work with echoes of ethnography and history but in which the verbatim reporting and use of information is fictionalised: the message and artistic provenance of the play transcend historical specificity. They believe that although ethnographic and verbatim theatres and their processes gave access to the materials, the difference between using and acknowledging people's original narratives and voices and fictionalising them places the project in a different orbit. It is a project that interacts critically with the material and encourages the audience to continue this dialogue in their engagement with the performance. One factor which Victor and Jumai faced, unlike any of the others, was that some of their research witnesses were also among their actors.

Witnesses playing witnesses creates a whole new ethnodrama game both for them and especially for their audiences as the problematic *Maybe one day when I'm famous* so painstakingly picked over already by its writer/researcher Johnny Saldaña and others, illustrates rather painfully but vividly. The audience of drama researchers were not informed that the actor playing Barry was in fact Barry. Ostensibly we were watching a young actor playing the part of 'Barry, a young and exceptionally talented actor'. What we were actually getting was Barry, a young actor playing 'a young actor' playing the part of 'Barry a young and exceptionally talented actor' – in other words Barry playing 'Barry' but with one crucial element missing: explicit manifestation of the talent of either Barry or 'Barry'. This is no slight to the performer; to be asked to demonstrate exceptional acting talent is a pretty hard task, probably beyond the capabilities of far more experienced actors than Barry. In addition he was doing this with material which was dramatic script-in-progress, not finished dramatic text that had been designed to give talent a platform for demonstration. The inevitable result for the audience was that when the real Barry was revealed at the end, the audience was gagged and some of us felt resentful. It was not that we had been conned, nor that we had felt it had been an unfair/unethical experience for Barry but we were unable to provide the critical and research feedback which was part of the purpose of watching the ethnodrama: this was because we did not want to hurt the feelings of the poor young man by revealing that one of the major themes of the play, his talent, had really been honoured in the breach rather than in his observance or our observation. Even writing this ten years later, we feel uncomfortable lest he feel put down if he reads this.

Alice had the most interesting opportunities to play with character and characterisation while risking neither authenticity nor infringement of either power or copyright, since they themselves were the central witnesses. Possibly conscious of the perils of self-representation in ethnodrama (at least one of them had seen *Maybe one day when I'm famous* and shared our response) they made an early decision to play each other, and to do so consistently: ie one actor played the same fictionalised character throughout. Typically they discussed this at length and reflected long and hard about it through the whole process, even writing data poems about it which they then enfolded into the performance itself in a multiple reflexivity. They went into the crafting of these embodiments of themselves carefully, both in the playwrighting, with Jane explicitly evoking Stanislavskian methods in writing her script segments and Prue doing the same in preparing herself for her performance.

Alice did represent other characters also, using various theatrical forms to embody them. The real voices of historical women academics became ghostly emanations in a damp cellar. The whole performance was kicked off by a fictional, stentorian and parodic male voice blaring over a public address system.

The commentator or 'researcher'

Alice also used an important device common in ethnodrama, and picked up by several of our contributors: 'The Researcher' as a character in the play. Their purpose was to frame the dramatised narrative as a reflexive research text. The Researcher's dialogue with the audience punctuated the central narrative, drawing attention to the team's research decisions in transforming ethnographic data into an embodied, aesthetic, performative form. This was the role Saldaña himself took in *Maybe someday when I'm famous*, though he does also see it as a 'problematic inclusion' (2005:18) as it was in that piece that, like Barry, he was playing 'himself'. Our contributor Jill also had misgivings. She scripted in The Researcher, whose role was to turn the dialogue to the key themes in the findings, a sensible purpose for a piece of research reporting. She felt the role was the least successful in performance, her rather half-hearted attempt at providing this character with dialogue probably mirroring her general ambivalence about inserting a researcher's voice into the action. Winnie from Hong Kong and her team embroidered the notion of researcher into 'detective', whose job is much the same: to investigate by collecting data and evidence, but who is more dramatically appealing. In their performance the detective used photos, tape recorder and suspicious materials to stimulate the audience's thought and reflections. For similar reasons of dramatic power and plausibility, as well as to convey expositional material, Linden fashioned some of her subsidiary data, taken from the transcript of the rail crash Inquiry, into the commentator roles of 'The Justice' and 'Psychologists'.

Richard also toyed with the idea of writing in a character called The Researcher, attracted by its potential to provide a distanced commentary. Unlike these other contributors, he rejected it on the advice of one of the teachers involved in the piece, who was concerned that as the play was to be student-centred this might intrude on and compromise their voice.

His decision to accede to the teacher's advice raises in two ways yet another interesting question about the relationship of the researcher-playwright to his or her sources, the witnesses of the ethnographic community. Of all our contributors Richard was the most meticulous member checker, and didn't leave it there. As his narrative indicates, his constant referral back to his witnesses became a major reflexive component of the play's development process. Here and on other occasions Richard indicates that he took the teachers' advice both on the pedagogical implications of his research for the students and on the writing itself. At times when one of them suggested that a particular incident 'would make a good scene for your play' his researcher self wondered if perhaps they were putting the cart before the horse but his dramatist's instinct was intrigued to find out what it was about the incident that rendered it as having dramatic potential. This automatically places those teachers in a kind of intermediate position: the students are his primary witnesses but the teachers are very much a part of the context of the setting, and as such, also informed insider witnesses, privileged ones. This cyclic reflexivity of research information he sustained with the students themselves, and this also had an effect on the aesthetics of the piece. Although none of the students suggested deletions of what he had written, several provided him with new information to *add* to the script, which they considered would clarify their thoughts and actions. For instance, one asked that Richard 'balance up his character' by including a more light-hearted scene based on data Richard had collected about him.

The paradox of ethnodrama

At whatever level they are working, all our contributors are absorbed in the challenges of transforming expository text into dramatic text. This paradoxically involves transforming the static into the moving and simultaneously transposing the moving into the fixed! The root of the paradox is something that ethnography and theatre share: both deal in attempting to record and communicate the transience and eva-nescence of human behaviour. Interview text is momentary, provi-sional and untrustworthy and the glimpses of a community's life granted to an ethnographer are partial, selective and to some extent always untypical. An ethnography is almost invariably a snapshot, rather than a movie; the ethnographer can usually only make images of ephemeral data, not track long-term developmental patterns. This is what theatre does too, but drama is usually structured in time asyn-chronously (with time re-arranged), to permit the depiction of the development of both narrative and character. Among Linden's frustra-tions was that most of her characters did not develop helpfully to the dramatist. The people who accidentally shared the Glenbrook rail crash were who they were. Fortunately, she was able to detect an implicit and gradually more explicit sense of community developing, not least among some of her own more or less randomly gathered group of wit-nesses, while they shared in the development of the art work about what brought them involuntarily together. She then had to deal with the narrative problem of immediacy. The witnesses' stories were retro-spective but she had to make them immediate for the audience: for this she could not rely on traditional dramatic structure either,since there was no crisis, climax or resolution to work for. The dramatic tension of the piece and any kind of recognisable ending had to be found else-where. On stage she had to translate the narratives collected *in situ* from seated participants who were not necessarily in a state of dramatic development into vivid and actively embodied dramatic action that would engage the audience.

She also had to deal with the obverse challenge of translating what she knew was evanescent interview data into 'fixed and transportable text' sufficiently to provide actors with a manageable and replicable script. As a researcher she had mistakenly approached the context of her re-search expecting some kind of grand narrative or coherent story. What she found was a lot of fragments which she had somehow to connect. The most naturally coherent emergent story among the bits was her own journey as a researcher from being positioned as a data gatherer to being what she describes as a 'privileged custodian'. With such a redolent tag attaching to her researcher self, it is surprising that, unlike several of our contributors, such as the scrap pickers, she did not choose to re-create herself in the play. She chose not to tell her story as a researcher, nor depict a fictionalised type. Perhaps she felt this would be intrusive in such an emotionally fraught context, and prefered to keep the hand of the researcher and that of the playwright/director hidden, manifest only in the artwork.

The whole question of maintaining an appropriate emotional distance and perspective between the researchers and their witnesses, and whatever is the appropriate distance of their audiences from either or both, is crucial to ethnodrama. It has an aesthetic and performative component that also had to be differently dealt with by our contributors, owing to their very diverse research sites and positions. The classic (and perhaps mythological) position of the detached and objective research observer is not available to the ethnodrama practitioner. In the research some measure of dispassionate distance may sometimes be available in the collection of observational record or third hand materials such as archives, though it is hard to imagine effective data being elicited without the researcher showing some sympathy towards the respondents. However, in developing and depicting a fictionalised representation of a community or a relationship, some measure of identification and empathy are essential, both to engage the audience and to represent with integrity the picture of the characters who make up the fictionalised community.

For some, like Richard, this was easy. The distance was a given, and conventional: he was a visiting artist/teacher in a school where he was known, working with classes of students through their own drama teachers, who were known and respected colleagues and all these relationships were standard and prescribed. He did not need or try to extend those norms. For Jill, as for other ethnodrama practitioners working in areas of health care involving trauma, extreme care about the distance of the researcher and the performance from the respondents: their data had to be taken and her aesthetically cautious decisions reflect this more than her inexperience. Her primary audience of colleagues and students encouraged her to take more risks than she had intended and her retrospective reflection is full of shrewd apprehension of where she might have been more aesthetically bold. Linden found herself making an involuntary journey from data gatherer to 'chronicler and privileged confidante'. She was perhaps not comfortable with this shortening distance since this phrase is omitted in her final draft, where she only acknowledges herself as a 'privileged custodian of their stories'.

At the other extreme it was a constant battle for Alice, depicting themselves, to find and maintain an appropriate aesthetic distance for their audience and for themselves and they constantly debated and renegotiated it, as in this telling vignette recorded from their discussions and also included in the show:

> Jane: I had your words and you were there, I felt awkward about that
>
> Kate: We weren't looking for a realistic interpretation of Chris
>
> Chris: Being an audience to your own story, all I could think was, 'Did I say that?' It felt a bit weird, but a positive weird and you did represent me.

Several of the contributors, notably the Hong Kong groups, mention the use of humour and irony as important distance markers. They also mention the deliberate use of non-naturalistic stylistic devices for this purpose. At various times in their case studies, many of the basic elements of drama are evoked to help define and regulate the distance between the researcher/performer, the respondents and the audiences: the fictionalised situation, the characters and characterisation, the language, the movement and gesture, space, time, dramatic tension, the symbols which emerged, the design and mise-en-scène. And of course the playwrighting itself: the aesthetic fashioning of raw words into embodied performance.

Conclusion

To sum up, we would like to juxtapose two powerful and contrasting statements about performance research which we find hard to better: one from a contributor to our case studies, one from the literature. They contrast, we suspect, not least because one of them is written by primarily a practitioner and a dramatic performer, the other by primarily a researcher and an ethnographer. The first is the insider's viewpoint of Kate from Hong Kong. Her testament as a whole, like all our contributors', exudes her and their excitement and enthusiasm for ethnodrama. But this passage encapsulates extraordinarily perceptively the tensions which have been at the centre of this chapter:

> This leads to one of my biggest issues, perhaps irresolvable, with ethnodrama for the purpose of performance to a chosen audience; the experience of watching an ethnographic performance can never replicate that of taking part in it. For the researcher/performers, creating such a performance is an outstanding way to analyse and internalize research findings. I can see that there might also be immense benefit to be gained on occasion from presenting the resulting performance to the research participants themselves, to create a unique dialectic between them and their researchers. However, an ethnodrama created to be performed for a third party will always be fraught. Not only will that third party audience have their experience of the drama limited to watching it but also the reality they are observing is fatally compromised. The ethnodrama will be the final product of various levels of interpretation: by participants of their own lives and of what they believe their researchers want to know about them and by the researcher and performers, of what constitutes participant 'epiphanies'.

On the other hand,

> Ethnotheatre reveals a living culture through its character-participants, and if successful, the audience learns about their world and what it's like to live in it... The collaborative power of performance and ethnography utilizes an embodied aesthetic practice coupled with the descriptive knowledge of lives and the conditions of living to stir up and provoke audiences to a critical social realisation and possible response. (Alexander, 2005:411)

No prizes for distinguishing the voice of the practitioner from the voice of the academic. Between them they encapsulate the hope and ambitions of performance research, and simultaneously the built-in ambiguity, ambivalence and contradiction inherent in the form which have been the subject of this book. In a way, the title of Kate's ethnodrama, *Scrap Pickers*, is also an elegant motif that sums up in its two words without grandiosity what this strange hybrid born of two worlds hopes to achieve.

SECTION B

CASE STUDIES

6

ALICE HOY IS NOT A BUILDING – WOMEN IN ACADEMIA

Jane Melissa Bird
Katriona Jane Donelan
Christine Sinclair
Prudence Wales

Introduction

In this chapter we look back on our enquiry into the nature of performance ethnography for researchers and practitioners. It is four years since we began. In this case study we highlight some of our discoveries, particularly those associated with two key decisions we made along the way: to be the researchers, performance-makers and performers in an ethnographic performance; and to include data drawn from our own lives as women educators at the University of Melbourne. In addition we have chosen to reflect the collaborative nature of our research in the writing of this chapter. We regard our involvement in this project as being of four individuals with different opinions, but after sustained consultation we have chosen to write as 'we'. And we have chosen to employ several different styles of writing within the chapter. We believe that this serves us well in our attempt to capture the discourse of researchers, performers and participants, both in the moment and on reflection. We use text boxes to highlight some of the dilemmas and questions which we grapple with still, even with the benefit of hindsight. We try to capture the nuances, uncertainties and challenges that arise in our ongoing researcher conversations.

In 2005 the four of us began our collective investigation of the relationship between performance and ethnographic research. We embarked on this project alongside our jobs as teachers, as post-graduate students, as academics and as women with family responsibilities. The primary research site for our ethnographic data collection and our performances was the University of Melbourne – a place of significance and connection for us all as current and former students and staff in the Faculty of Education.

This collaborative project was our response to the burgeoning interest in 'the deeply intertwined relationship between doing ethnography and producing artistic work' (Goldman, 2007:832). We saw performance ethnography as an orientation to research that related directly to our skills and experiences as drama educators and theatre makers. Like many practitioner-researchers within performance studies, we were drawn to Conquergood's vision of performance ethnography as a way of knowing and a mode of understanding, as well as a method of critical inquiry (1991:187). Yet we also sensed a potential tension between the aesthetic demands of theatrical performance and the nature and purposes of ethnographic research. We were aware of many educational and social researchers with no drama background enthusiastically and uncritically embracing performance to present research findings. So we began our project with open questions about the place of the aesthetic in the research processes and the products of 'ethnographic performance'. Our aims were to study the uses of drama in ethnographic data analysis, and to explore the consequences of using theatre form to represent and communicate ethnographic research findings.

We asked each other ...

...as we embarked on our investigation, questioning the place of an aesthetic within the presentation of research findings:

Could an ethnographic performance be engaging and entertaining... have a plot or storyline ... apply dramatic elements such as contrast, symbol, mood, tension and climax ... and provide an authentic interpretation of our data?

And, if so, how could we house our data within a dramatic plot or narrative?

Do we have a shared conceptual understanding of what constitutes aesthetic work, entertaining theatre and good research?

We continue to grapple with these and other questions as we come to terms with the nature of our collaboration as well as multiple notions of the aesthetic.

Questions and themes

We focused our ethnographic performance research on women educators' experiences of tertiary institutions in the past and present, specifically at the University of Melbourne. Early on we gathered in the Education Faculty's drama studio, after a day of teaching, to interview each other about our experiences of education. We each responded to the question: 'How did you get here?' These collective interviews generated multi-layered narratives about women's relationships with tertiary education, about interconnected personal and professional roles and multiple and competing tasks and agendas. As the project proceeded we generated and collected other data, including historical data about women educators at the teacher's college that was amalgamated with the university twenty years ago. Our data analysis revealed themes of vulnerability, powerlessness and marginalisation for women within tertiary educational institutions, as well as collaboration, resilience, persistence and passion for learning and teaching. Our ongoing lived experiences as academics and graduate students in the university at a time of major institutional changes – academic reviews, staffing cuts, restructuring and major building works – resonated with and crystallised these emergent themes.

As a group we saw ourselves as collaborative ethnographers, co-performers and storytellers who, in anthropologist Ruth Behar's terms, told 'stories about real people in real places' (Behar, 2008:530). Our project involved fieldwork at the university, collective interviews, drama-based analysis, transformation of data into dramatic form, the devising and construction of a theatrical performance, rehearsals and forums with audiences. For over three years we generated hundreds of hours of taped discussions, piles of transcribed interviews, field notes, reflective journal entries, photographs, historical documents, data matrices, character and plot outlines, multiple versions of scripts and an ethnographic performance text called *Alice Hoy is Not a Building*.

Our ethnographic performance project opened up a number of methodological questions, some of which we referred to directly or alluded to metaphorically and symbolically in our performance text. According to Alexander 'performance ethnography' is 'literally the staged re-enactment of ethnographically derived notes' (2005:411). While mindful of this, we examined the consequences of moving beyond a literal staging of ethnographically derived notes, of creating a fictional narrative to house our emergent themes. We discussed at length the potential or perceived tension between what Saldaña calls 'an ethnodramatist's ethical obligation to recreate an authentic representation of reality (thus enhancing fidelity) and the license for artistic interpretation of that reality (thus enhancing the aesthetic possibilities)' (2005:32). For us, the notion of reality in the transformation of ethnographic data into performance needed further interrogation. We questioned the assumption that researchers discover a reality that is independent of their construction and mediation of it through discourse, narrative and performance.

We generated methodological questions as we worked dramatically with our data and constructed the performance text. We were influenced by the pioneering work of Turner (1982) and Schechner (1985) who see performance ethnography as a way of representing cultural practices and cultural others through embodied presentation. The auto-ethnographic dimensions of our project as it evolved were initially problematic for some of us. However, we found that the interweaving of personal stories and biographical data with oral history and historical documents illuminated complex socio-cultural themes underlying the experiences of diverse women within tertiary education. We analysed this ethnographic material largely through the processes of performance making, through embodying the storied experiences in the interview data and the historical records.

The performance text

Our performance text, *Alice Hoy is Not a Building*, focuses on three women's relationships with each other in a context of institutional crisis and change. Through its form and content, we highlighted the key themes, the questions and the tensions that we identified in the data, as well as our meta-commentary as researchers. To frame the dramatised narrative as a reflexive research text we constructed the character of 'The Researcher', whose dialogue with the audience punctuates the central narrative, drawing attention to our research decisions in transforming ethnographic data into an embodied, aesthetic, performative form. In this way we signalled to the audience that as researchers we were shaping the performed meaning of the ethnographic data from our particular personal, cultural, ontological and theoretical frameworks.

Yet, as we shaped our play, we questioned ...

...the choices we made as researchers, performers and playbuilders and the meanings they generated.

If we were to include four researchers in the narrative, how could we move between performing the 'characters' in the central plot and representing our research selves, commenting on the action?

If instead, we constructed a single 'Researcher', how could one character/one actor represent us all, four women researchers with diverse specialisations, ideas, approaches and opinions?

If we created one character to 'represent us all' what ethical questions would this raise about representation?

The character of the 'Researcher', a representation of us all, did raise ethical questions about representations of ourselves and our research, notions of merging characters and opinions and playing with the ways we constructed meaning, an ongoing tension we continue to feel uneasy about.

Luttrell sees ethnography as a 'social art form' and one that is 'creative, inventive, emotionally charged, and uneasy' (2000:520). Our dynamic and demanding group processes enabled us to challenge, debate and contest our varied interpretations of our ethnographic data. Through intensive discussions and our embodied explorations in workshops, we analysed the relationships between women's lived experiences and the politics of education within an academic institution from our different perspectives. As the project proceeded we found that our knowledge of a shared performance language generated unexpected interpretative insights into the data. We constructed a performance text that we felt represented our multiple views rather than one unified group response to the data.

We have shared *Alice Hoy is Not a Building* with the Melbourne University community in our drama studio next to the Alice Hoy Building. We have also presented it at a national drama conference in Sydney, at an arts education research symposium, at the World Congress of Drama/Theatre and Education in Hong Kong and at the Fourth International Congress of Qualitative Inquiry in America. We regard each performance event as an opportunity to further our inquiry through our dialogues with audiences. Each new context requires us to adapt aspects of the performance text, to modify some of our aesthetic decisions in response to the space, the audience and the social and cultural context.

Our aim is to communicate our research findings about women's relationships to the University of Melbourne and about the process of doing ethnographic performance through our collaboratively devised performance text. We use theatre form and dramatic narrative to shape and embody the ethnographic data and to represent the stories, themes, questions and issues that emerged for us. The play provides our meta-commentary on our investigations into a research process that is both ethnographic and performative.

Generating data

Central to this project has been our ethnographic inquiry into the educational journeys of women, their experiences of tertiary education at the university and the former teachers' colleges that were located on the site. Our plan at the outset was to conduct open-ended ethnographic interviews with different women associated with the university. We began by devising a series of questions and trialled them on each other.

Deep space

The drama room is in the basement, hot in summer and freezing in winter. In here, the four women meet with their prepared set of questions and their tape recorder. They pull four chairs out into the middle of the space, and place the tape recorder on a cylindrical drama block in the middle. On the table in the corner of the room sits the kettle, the cups, teabags and milk. They share a cup of tea and some meandering conversation before they begin.

On this night, the women discover what they come to call 'deep space'. Kate agrees to be the first interviewee. Chris follows. They begin with the question 'How did you get here?' Slowly, the room becomes smaller, just large enough to hold four women as they become immersed in the stories shared. One question leads to another. The interviewers sense when to ask the next question and who should ask it: there is no turn-taking as such. The sweep of rich and complex lives is played out in stories told and not told, in the laughter and the silences. Time is held at bay in this deep space where trust is fundamental and the line between intimacy and disclosure is understood.

Our interview transcripts contained rich themes, revealing the educational, emotional, professional and physical journeys we each made to the University of Melbourne. They opened up questions for us about the lived experiences of women as learners and teachers on this site and about the intertwined personal and professional roles they play. As the project continued we generated further data by writing individual and collaborative field notes and recording our ongoing experiences of teaching, studying and working at the university at a time of change. We also examined historical data from the university website, oral history texts and archives. In particular we focused on Alice Hoy (1893-1976), a notable female leader of the university who did much to shape the future of teacher training and educational research in Victoria. Our group interview questions also guided our exploration of the historical data and the words, images, symbols and stories of women who attended the university in the past.

Many times we ask...

Do we have enough data, do we have too much data?

Do we have data from enough sources? How will we collect more data? When?

What will we do with it when we have it?

More questions, more concerns:

If we focus on the verbatim data from ourselves will our work become inward looking, self-congratulatory, self-absorbed, and not good ethnography?

If we continue to collect data, using interviews with others at the University, how do we select our participants; on what basis do we limit our data collection; how do we find the time?

Do we need to all conduct the interviews?

Could we do a *vox pop*, capturing snapshots of other voices, other experiences of women at the university? (and when?)

One of us would argue to conduct more interviews, another would advocate that we continue to explore the data we had – 'Let's set aside our concerns about whether this is the right way to do performance ethnography', someone suggested.

As we explored our own material we encountered layers of meaning that echoed beyond ourselves, and resonance with the experiences of others we knew who worked at the university, themes repeated themselves from one interview transcript to the next. Perhaps we could use this data as our foundation and maintain our commitment to ethnographic rigour?

Performance-based data analysis

We analysed the transcribed interviews and historical data using performative processes. As a group of drama educators with skills and knowledge of performance making we drew on our shared repertoire of drama techniques to explore data-based stories and emerging themes. Often working in pairs, we constructed images and scenes to represent our interpretations of the material and performed these to each other. This approach was driven by our desire to undertake detailed analysis of the data through dramatic exploration and simultaneously to construct a dynamic, engaging and informative performance text.

Workshop 1: Experimenting with data analysis

The women sat in a circle and read through two interviews' transcripts, quoting aloud amusing or interesting passages. Chris took the lead; she directed the group to work in pairs, examine the transcripts to select a story or theme to present through performance to the other pair. There was no discussion about this process; they all knew what to do.

Armed with highlighters and pens, Kate and Jane discussed themes in Chris's interview transcript, highlighting sections of the text. They moved towards the positive stories, acknowledging that these were the words of their friend and in this first workshop session they were going to be cautious. They scribbled down verbatim words from the transcript. They created a visual map of the various stories related to key decisions along Chris's educational journey.

Then, they created a physical representation of their map, using their bodies and then moving across the space. At different places in the space they paused and spoke selected words, and recreated moments of stories related to that place. Jane used mainly physical actions, and Kate was one step behind speaking verbatim text, layering a reflective tone over each event. Through improvising they explored the motivations behind each step in the journey; in this way they could physically explore the options before a choice was made. They then choreographed their improvised ideas, refining the speed of actions and clarifying their physical expressions and use of the space; at one point Jane moved backwards as if being sucked into a decision. Single words, phrases and snippets of the stories they had selected from the transcript were spoken with the movements. Even though they originally decided to avoid the difficult themes in Chris' transcript, through the use of non-naturalistic movement and symbolic action the performance exposed some of the struggles and crisis points of her journey.

They performed their scene to Chris and Prue. Jane felt a level of discomfort presenting this material to Chris, as this was her story.

Jane:	*I had your words and you were there, I felt awkward about that.*
Kate:	*We weren't looking for a realistic interpretation of Chris*
Chris:	*Being an audience to your own story, all I could think was, 'Did I say that?' It felt a bit weird, but a positive weird and you did represent me.*

Prue and Chris focused on Kate's transcript. They highlighted key sections of the transcript describing her physical journey, her clothes, her body image, the hectic car trip, multi-tasking and complexities of the working day. They also selected images of her life when she was a student at Melbourne University. Images of twin sets and pearls contrasting with kaftans and share houses, grabbed Prue's and Chris's attention. They decided to create two 'Kates', to be performed simultaneously: a young Kate reflecting on her student life and an older Kate reflecting on her daily journey to work at the university.

Jane and Kate became the audience to their interpretation of the transcript. Physically the older Kate was contained to one side of the space at home and then in her car recalling and re-enacting her trip to university that morning. The domestic and personal detail of her everyday life related to the selected themes. In a parallel space, the younger Kate stood and reflected on her life – the story of how the alternative lifestyle of the 1960s influenced and changed the girl who had arrived at university wearing 'twin sets and pearls'. A lively discussion followed:

> Kate: *I don't think it was just about me, it was also reflecting a time.*

The contrasting images presented through parallel storytelling, through stillness and silence as a character looks into an imaginary mirror, and through comic timing – when a character teeters on the edge of a crack in the floor – revealed layers of meaning in the data. The reflective sessions between performers and audience allowed for feedback and further analysis of the themes and images presented in the short performances. This process allowed us to air our individual feelings as we witnessed our own stories being represented, transformed and reconstructed by other group members. By encouraging the participant/ interviewee to respond to the interpretation of her words, a sense of trust developed and it became possible for each of us to accept or reject other performance ideas in future workshop sessions. Our records of these short workshop scenes evolved into scripts that became the basis of our performance text. The outcome of our first workshop encouraged us to continue with a performance-based approach. Consequently, the nature of our data grew. Dramatic exploration and performance making became central to our data analysis and to the production of new data. As we analysed our primary data we generated more data from our discussions. These led to verbal and physical interpretations, improvisations and reflections, which were then refined and developed further.

Over a series of 27 workshop sessions we continued to analyse the transcribed interviews and historical primary data, identifying questions, categories and themes. We used a range of performance techniques including improvisation, character development, role play, symbolism, manipulation of dramatic elements, scriptwriting and rehearsal processes to explore and transform verbatim data. Space, contrast, conflict, climax, timing, tension, mood, rhythm, sound, symbol, focus and language were used to provoke intellectual and emotional responses in the audiences. Rather than relying on a reading of the selected verbatim text, as performer-researchers we manipulated the space, the actors and dramatic elements to construct an interpretation of the data and our research findings through our theatrical text. Our personal stories, dreams and nightmares, interpretations and reflections all found their way into the play and prompted questions for us: what then was fact and what was fiction? Where did the data stop and the fiction enter? As a result, our selection of text was influenced by our capacity to choose images that would translate well into a physical representation and that most effectively embodied a given theme. We examined stories that highlighted one participant's experiences within a tertiary institution and then, through physical action, suggested themes that were pertinent to this woman's educational and professional journey and were also resonant for other women educators and their journeys.

Our multiple roles as actors, performance makers and audience members provided 'a method of both understanding self and other, and self as other while engaging in performance' (Alexander, 2005:433). We analysed the data from inside as performers and from outside as audience and performance makers. As Carlson points out, the reflexive qualities of performance can inform the ethnographer's processes of investigation as it 'involves a consciousness of doubleness' (1996:5). Through performance reflexivity we developed an embodied understanding of the data and also responded to the evolving text from an audience perspective. Our drama-based workshops provided a site for a dialogic approach to analysing and interpreting the data and a cyclical and critical approach to performance making.

The performance text

Alice Hoy is Not a Building focuses on the interactions of three women within a stressful and rapidly changing institutional environment: a senior academic, Alice; her junior colleague, Rose; and her doctoral student, Faith, who teaches at an inner city school. The story of these three women and their lives at the university centres on a single, difficult day involving an office relocation, disruption of teaching, physical demolition of buildings and the dismantling of a drama department, its archives and its courses.

Performing the play: Part One

Room 419 of the Creative Arts Building at the University of Melbourne is a long room with high ceilings and a warm vibe. The audience is diverse. Many are friends and colleagues who have heard murmurings of this play for some time. Others are more distant: members of the education faculty or the wider education community who have been invited or who have been drawn to this event by its description.

The play begins with sound and vision from the data projector. The four women performers, seated on the chairs set to one side of the performance area, look expectantly at the audience and at the stacked step ladder, centre stage, the symbolic representation of the absent Professor Frank Worthy. As the leader of the research team, he is about to present their research findings in ground-breaking ethnographic research.

Frank's disembodied voice booms out over the heads of the audience, in a self-aggrandising welcome to the research community which has come to hear about his research project. Quickly, Frank's presentation begins to unravel. It becomes evident that Frank has perhaps not been as hands-on in this research project as he may have suggested in his introduction. He makes his excuses and leaves the women researchers and their audience to their own devices.

So ends the prologue for the real play. The women take charge of the space and the presentation of the research. One woman comments:

> All the fucker had to do was introduce us.

The four researchers, Prue, Kate, Jane and Chris move quickly to re-define the space, the sound of ripping masking tape signalling the marking out of the performance territory, a square to provide a central

92

point of focus for actors and audience. Jane comes to Chris with instructions and a variety of props, as she is inducted into the role of The Researcher. As the other women take their positions for the beginning of the real play, The Researcher poses the first question the women asked in their interviews, and a PowerPoint appears:

How did you get here?

As researchers we are also performing

We approached this project as researchers and performers, teachers and students, friends and colleagues. We felt we knew each other when, armed with highlighters and pens, we began analysing our stories and mapping out our accidental journeys. When we began to perform incidents and anecdotes from our interviews it felt awkward to re-present someone we knew and 'a bit weird' to be watching re-presentations of ourselves. As signalled in a data poem that we included in the performance, we began to question our knowledge and understanding of each other.

I am being you, who I think I know,
but actually
when I'm there,
in the body,
I don't know you at all.

Through our performance-based research our bodies operated as sites of knowledge. Inscribed with past experiences, our bodies held the 'archives', to use Nicholson's term (2003), from which we generated research data and worked collectively. As performers of our research text we shaped ideas during our rehearsal processes with our individual/collective bodies, using and seeking a variety of methods to embody aspects of the data. We analysed and interpreted data cognitively, corporally and figuratively. In doing so, our understanding of our research project grew and seeped through our skin, into our bodies to be reassembled, restored and reinscribed. These enacted embodiments of each other were constructed assemblages through which we explored our ideas, thoughts and feelings about our research inter-subjectively.

We used drama processes not only as a way to communicate our research but also as essentially an act of discovery. As a kinaesthetic and cognitive form, drama communicates with an audience on multiple levels: visually, aesthetically, emotionally, and cerebrally. As performers we drew on the process of learning that underlies the way in which many actors approach their craft: intuitively, self-reflexively, through observation and research, and through the individual informing the collective.

Many researchers acknowledge the parallels between drama and qualitative research (Turner and Bruner, 1986; Courtney, 1990). Henry (2000: 51) draws a comparison between a playscript and a research text in the use of figurative language to convey meaning in both forms. Our performance text contained images, metaphors and symbols drawn from the data stories and interviews. Our performative bodies symbolically struggled to climb an ivy covered wall, to bend down and search for keys, and to flex into knots to locate a signal so the mobile phone would work in a crisis. In our exploration of the roles of women at the University of Melbourne we enacted and embodied that institution's procedures and systems of control. Simultaneously, our bodies became sites of 'revolt' and 'ethical responsibility' (Davies *et al*, 2005:344); through the act of performance we rebelled against the place of women in a patriarchal workplace and sought to analyse how social and professional spaces affected us.

Probyn (2003) claims that auto-ethnography recognises the body as 'a site for the production of knowledge, feelings, emotions and history, all of which are central to subjectivity'. As the central character, Alice, justifies 'trying to get another day out of her work shirt' she not only conveys the daily demands of her life but also a sense of rebellion against what is deemed to be proper and conventional behaviour. Our embodiment of each other's stories gave us access to our individual and collective knowledge, experiences, beliefs, and sentiments and enabled us to inscribe our bodies with new understandings. The performance strategies we used allowed us to connect theory with embodied knowledge.

Our performance of each other's stories led to new acts of discovery as we came to know each other in new and distinct ways. As four experienced drama educators we shared a kinaesthetic understanding of our art form, despite the fact that, prior to *Alice Hoy*, it was some time since we had performed to an audience. We each prepared for performing a constructed character and speaking the words extracted from the ethnographic data in very different ways. Prue spent considerable time before and after the public performances getting in and out of character. Although happy to set up props she needed quiet while she focused and became irritated when interrupted. She adopted a Stanislavskian approach, implementing emotional recall, working her lines and locating her character until she physically felt her presence in her body. Jane drew on Stanislavski's system during the scriptwriting phase; conscious of her character's motivation, consistency and objectives, she often asked about her character's through-line and super-objective. At the beginning of each performance, Jane sat in view of the audience stage right and appeared to go into a deep space to find her character. Kate found her character through the verbatim language within the script, picking up the character's speech rhythms and nuances as she spoke her lines while setting up chairs or placing props and belongings to the side of the room. Chris, who privileged her director self over herself as an actor, struggled for some time with the group's indecisiveness about how to represent the researchers' perspectives in the text. Once The Researcher emerged as a clearly defined character, Chris used objects associated with the act of doing ethnographic research: highlighter pens, sticky labels, notepads and tape recorders to refine and develop her performance.

We ask, 'how'?

We sit around a table talking about how we see ourselves and each other as researchers: ethnographer, neophyte researcher, post-post structuralist, adventurer, explorer, warrior queen. For the longest time we embrace the image of Boadicea the ancient warrior queen as our motif for the researcher; and we also play with the notion of the film-noir detective, uncovering the mysteries of our research questions in back alleys and on dark nights. But how to stage this within the context of the narrative we have developed around the three women?

And how to perform it?

Perhaps we are trivialising the research function or underplaying it or distracting from the central narrative?

We brought the questions of representing the research to each performance and back into the rehearsal studio afterwards. Audiences engaged with us on the questions, told us what they saw and how they constructed meaning, and we adapted. Boadicea, or 'Bowie', laden with props and costumes to suggest different phases of research, ultimately became The Researcher, watching the ethnography come to life, providing commentary, operating sound equipment where necessary, building a relationship with the audience and ultimately, with the other performers. We still continue to discuss this role – wondering perhaps if our next step might be to physically position the research embodied in the form of The Researcher centre stage, in the midst of the action, rather than on the side, watching.

Performing the play: Part Two

The audience is introduced to three women, Alice, Faith and Rose, all making their way to the University. In direct address to the audience they reflect on their professional and personal journeys. The Researcher sits at her desk, to the side, setting up her work space, listening to her taped interviews, making notes on her computer, and occasionally referring to the action on stage, reflecting the early data gathering of the four women whom she represents. At key moments, the action on stage freezes and she speaks directly to the audience, offering a commentary on the progress of the researchers. As she speaks, the data projector adds a visual and textual layer to the event through PowerPoint headings.

The story of the three women and their lives at the university begins to unfold. Address to the audience as a theatrical device is used less and less as the characters become more enmeshed in the playing out of a single, difficult day. The sounds of jackhammers herald relocation and potential dislocation.

Through all phases of the play-making and research process, we struggled with negotiating through our individual ideas, and there were times for each of us when we had to compromise. This raised questions about how far we should go. How long should we argue a point? How long should we be willing to listen when we didn't understand what another was talking about? When should we remain silent for the greater good of the group? Was silence an act of responsibility to self, or the group, or was it a cop-out? Did silence mean our acceptance, concurrence, agreement or was it something else, like frustration, disappointment or even anger? We also deliberated, individually and as a group, over when we should let go of ideas we wanted to include and also how long we should struggle and try to make them work? Our decisions were based variously on the practical and/or emotional and/or aesthetic.

Collaboration or compromise?

Collaboration is not an easy process, particularly if it is a truly democratic process which we are committed to. We all engage in negotiation; in compromise, at some time.

When a scene is tedious but you feel the information is important, how do you find a form to make it interesting? In one scene, we all have monologues. We struggle in each rehearsal to find ways to present them for weeks. Eventually, we give a rehearsal over to workshopping. Who suggests this? Instead of monologues, we experiment with a game of 'secret agents' which is drawn from the data. The monologues are cut, merged and interspersed into dialogue and childhood games, a stylised and playful scene.

Compromise, we discover, is about many things: negotiating, letting go, fighting for, staying silent, taking on board, and sometimes about allowing something that is important to someone else to go ahead.

Aesthetic decisions

In the drama room we manipulated form and content, guided by our various (not always shared) understandings of the ethnographic data and the need to achieve a satisfying theatre aesthetic. The tensions that we encountered, within the group, and collectively with the project, required us to confront not only the dilemmas that all artists face as they transform data into their chosen aesthetic form, but the inherent tensions within performance ethnography itself.

Performing the play: Part Three

For an audience of teachers, university staff and students there is much to identify with. There is laughter of recognition as Faith drops her keys down the lift shaft at her school and is told that she must wait a month for replacement. Alice's impossibly tight schedule and her willingness to move her first meeting to 6am also prompts response to the absurdity or perhaps in recognition of the familiar.

> Alice: No I could get up at five. Let's say Brunetti's at six. Oh, they're not open that early? Of course...

Alice's office is relocated without notice. This brings a disruption in mood and style in the play. The Removalist rips the masking tape from the floor – the definition of space is temporarily suspended.

The legitimacy of humour

Is it okay to be funny? In our offices, there is laughter, ironic sometimes, desperate and a little manic occasionally.

In the studio, we wonder about the humour and playfulness in our play. Even while we laugh through rehearsals, replaying moments of our lives, we ask:

If this scene is funny, is it a legitimate way to interpret data and construct meaning?

Can our serious research intentions be captured in slapstick? Our central character Alice tries to get a signal on her phone, in her basement office – she climbs onto a table, contorts her body as a human aerial while attempting to obtain information about a critical meeting.

The Building Supervisors, in gentle parody of the *Keystone Cops meet Abbot and Costello*, move furniture, establish the boundaries of newly allocated space and demonstrate a blissful ignorance of the consequences to the women of decisions made beyond their reach and their control.

We discover the serious in the funny and the funny in the serious and wonder if we can capture this in our play.

Performing the play: Part Three ... continued

The story lurches from absurdity, with playful subversive moments of clowning, to magic realism as Rose finds herself in a basement and begins to hear the voices of women from the past emanating from the walls. The Researcher interposes, reminding the audience of the challenges that the play has presented to the four researchers she represents. She performs the sending of an email to Laurel Richardson, mentor and commentator on alternative forms of research reporting.

What is legitimate data?

she asks Laurel.

When The Researcher asks:

Can we improvise?

we are signalling our questioning of the constraints and boundaries of performance ethnography. We had discovered the research potential of improvising with verbatim data, immersing ourselves in an aesthetic experience of the ethnographic material, reaching for expressive and symbolic ways to explore and understand what had been said and also what had been left unsaid by participants. Yet we remained concerned that our reach for an aesthetic and intuitive artistic process might over-whelm or distort the methodological integrity of our ethnographic research practice.

During the data analysis phase of our project, Laurel Richardson visited the University of Melbourne and we held a long conversation with her about our work, about the nature of ethnographic performance and other creative analytic practices (Richardson, 2000:929). Richardson's response to our questions about the legitimacy of our drama-based approach to data analysis reassured us and informed our own emerging exploration of ethnographic performance as a research practice.

Richardson refers to the reconstruction of the sense of an event in ethnographic drama. Our decision to extend our data collection to archival materials, images and stories of women who had attended the university in the past brought further aesthetic challenges. How could we go beyond simply cataloguing the experiences of women of the past, whose educational journeys mirrored or contrasted with our own? What meanings could we construct from the verbatim material, the photographs and the stories of these women? And how could the understanding we gained through this process be represented in our play?

Performing the play: Part Four

A new office, in some dusty remote basement room, is established for Alice. It is signified by one of the actors marking out a tiny square on the stage, using a tape dispenser with bright yellow tape marked 'Fragile'.

As the audience is invited into the basement with Alice, Rose and Faith, the play opens out: stories of many women who have studied at the university in the past provide a dramatic backdrop to the central and invented plot line of the three main characters trying to get through a very difficult day. Both characters and audience are faced with the question of how the past frames the present, particularly in the context of the evolving history of women attending the university, encountering experiences of invisibility and vulnerability within an unwieldy and unforgiving institution. Against this backdrop, the character of Alice Hoy is introduced not in the flesh but in the form of a portrait projected onto the wall.

In our performance text the invisible women of the past are represented as disembodied voices that the central characters hear when they find themselves in the basement of their building. In the space between action and audience the multiple meanings that are suggested by these voices, and by the ambiguous responses to them by Rose, Faith and Alice contributes to the inter-textuality of the performance. Bringing together images, music, verbatim text, video, data projection and the interplay of live and recorded human voice and bodies in space evokes the interrelationships and disjunctions we had discovered through our research and invites audience members in to form their own interpretations.

Performing the play: Part Five

The play builds to its climax. In an orchestrated sequence of mobile phone calls and parallel dialogue, tension mounts. Against a surreal display of opening and closing doors, projected onto the back wall, the audience is presented with Alice's worst nightmare: she has missed an important meeting and her drama courses will be cut and staff will be lost. The audience is silent. There is a collective intake of breath as Alice returns to her office, close to complete collapse. The ghost of Alice Hoy offers some unexpected advice.

In the closing moments of the play, Rose returns to Alice's office. In the face of Alice's imminent collapse, the younger woman reminds herself, Alice and the audience, of the significance of the mentor and role model to her life at the university.

Rose: *Oh, Alice. You're the last ...you're the last person to let me down Alice. (long pause) Come on, let's go.*

Representing the researchers in performance

How do we create a character who represents us all, from the inside? We can name the kinds of researchers we are or aspire to be, and we can describe some of our actions, but we have such different experiences of this research journey, such different perceptions. I am only privy to my own experiences and perceptions, and to the publicly declared understandings, perceptions and behaviours of my collaborators – I sense their experience, but am reluctant to represent an approximation of what I think it might be. (Chris, reflecting on the Melbourne performance, June 2007).

We resolved that it was important to find multi-textual and embodied ways to reflect our research process, within and alongside the plot and characters of our play. We decided that Chris would become the embodiment of the four researchers, placed on the stage, but separate from the dramatic creation of the lives of the women in the story. We then incorporated data projections of our research questions, significant quotations, photographic and video images, data poems and moments when the actors inside the play stepped outside of the action. In this way we made physical the shifting positioning of participant researchers.

The theatrical representation of ourselves as researchers, through the character of Bowie, The Researcher prompted many questions and responses from audiences. We continued to reflect on and adjust our representation of the researchers, prompted in part by Chris's need, as the actor, for clarity of purpose and function of the character. Our understanding of The Researcher as a device in the performance is still evolving:

Perhaps we made a fundamental mistake in our conception of Bowie. Perhaps there was no need to represent us all – all the different kinds of researchers we were during the research. Perhaps we should have tackled the task of representing the research, not the researchers. (Chris, June 2007)

101

As we continue to grapple with the aesthetic demands of capturing our experiences as researchers in a dramatic form, we discover again the reflexivity of the process: we seek yet one more refinement of The Researcher's role in the play and make new discoveries about the nature of performance ethnography as a compelling and emerging form of qualitative research.

Performing the play: Part Six

The final moments of the performance see the actors reprising their opening lines (signalling that their lives continue) and the Researcher taking centre stage, framing the question that resonates for characters and researchers alike:

*Where do **we** go next?*

The audience

Making the choice to explore and present research through drama processes and performance opens up rich possibilities for dialogue with the audience. Each time we perform *Alice Hoy is Not a Building* we ask audience members to construct their own meanings of the play and its meta-commentary on research. After our performance we invite audience members to participate in a reflective critique about the characters, the aesthetic form, the issues it raises about women within a tertiary institution, and doing performance ethnography.

Victim or heroine?

Some audience members have suggested that we had produced a victim narrative. Others said they regarded the play as a hero narrative. Can it be both? How do audience members come to such different meanings?

At the 2008 International Congress on Qualitative Research, Caroline Ellis said that she regarded auto-ethnographies as neither victim nor hero narratives. On the contrary, they were about survival and should be considered as survivor narratives.

But we continue to wonder about the meanings made from our performed stories? Can we control those perceptions of victim or heroine, through performance? Do we want to?

In our ongoing investigation we have discovered that the role of the audience is critical. The development and construction of a research outcome that is not only aesthetic in nature, but temporal, dynamic and dialogic, recreated anew each time it is performed, invites a re-consideration of the processes of interpretation and analysis that lie at the heart of all research. Each audience is different, bringing different understandings of the content and the aesthetic form: each person is influenced by their own experiences, background and their relation-ships with the performers. This was highlighted when we first presented the play at he University of Melbourne to an audience of family and friends, followed by a performance to academics and researchers from across the university, many from the Faculty of Education.

Our various dialogues with audiences have given us, as researcher/performers, important insights into how our play connects with, pro-vokes, challenges and possibly alienates a particular audience. Each time we perform, we give careful consideration to how we will frame the post-performance interactions with audience members to provide an appropriate forum for them to respond and also to allow space for us, as performer/researchers to engage with these responses. Our inter-pretations continue to evolve through each performance cycle. In each rendition of *Alice Hoy is Not a Building* we generate new data, discover new meanings and nuances in our interpretations of each other and ask new questions. Where do we go from here?

7

ENCOUNTERS IN CHILD CARE

Jill Robinson

I must make a confession right at the start. Unlike many of the contributors to this book, I am a heath professional and educator who has tried to use a dramatic form to bring my research findings into the classroom. I am a novice and have undertaken this project with a meagre repertoire of experience in the dramatic arts. Some of what I say about the processes I describe will appear clumsy and naïve and some of the early problems would have been avoided had I thought to engage the expertise of drama scholars. Nevertheless, as I start to use my script as a learning tool in the classroom, it is increasingly clear that the final product of my clumsy progress is having an impact and initiating a response in the classroom that suggests it has fully engaged those who took part. What I have tried to do here is to reveal the nuts and bolts of creating a Reader's Theatre script from verbatim research data. In doing so I have reflected on some of the dilemmas, tensions and opportunities that working in this medium have highlighted.

How I came to use my data to produce a Reader's Theatre script for performance in the classroom is not straightforward. The research upon which it is based was undertaken at the University of East Anglia by myself and a researcher, Julie Young. It began in March 2004 as an ordinary evaluation of four care co-ordination schemes in one county in the UK that aimed to improve services for children with complex needs and their families. These schemes were mainly established in response to problems identified in the extant UK system which a government green paper at the time had described as 'often poorly co-ordinated', where 'accountability is unclear' and where 'information is not shared between agencies so that warning signs are not recognised and acted upon' (DfES/DH, 2003:21). Each scheme shared a common intention to establish better care co-ordination in order to address these problems and provide improved more integrated services for children with disabilities who had complex needs. Most schemes were based on the provision of key workers who would mediate between the family and the service providers and provide a 'clear point of reference for the family' (DfES, 2002:16).

The evaluation strategy was designed to be formative and predominantly qualitative and to assist future development by exploring the experiences and perceptions of parents and key workers involved in the schemes, identifying areas of good practice for wider dissemination and describing the range of problems associated with implementation. Our data were generated predominantly through in-depth interviews with parents, interviews both individual and group with key workers and a small survey of parents. The findings and consequent recommendations were disseminated to funders and their key stakeholders in a relatively conventional formal report with executive summary (Young and Robinson, 2005).

The idea of using performance-based forms of data display came to me slowly over a period that roughly coincided with the care co-ordination evaluation project. It began when I attended a conference in September 2004 on 'Narrative Research in Health and Illness' in London, September 2004, where I participated in a workshop run by Susan Cox and Jeff Nisker entitled *Exploring the ethics of researching and presenting stories of genetic risk through Reader's Theatre, thought experiments, found poetry and photography*, on the ethics of portraying genetically inherited illness narratives. In this workshop we performed a Reader's Theatre script written by Jeff Nisker, using the narrative accounts of women who had close female relatives who had died of a particularly aggressive hereditary form of breast cancer. As a participant, I was struck by the emotional power of reading or hearing the words of women who were trying to articulate what it was like to have your mother and aunt die before they were 40 and face the likelihood of an early death yourself. As a health professional, stories of this kind were not unfamiliar to me; but there was something real and immediate about experiencing them as a Reader's Theatre performance and I started to consider its potential as an educational tool for health professionals.

The idea of Reader's Theatre originated in schools as a way of improving children's reading and understanding of literature (Shepard, 1994). Typically it involves a performance to an audience of a script that is read rather than learned, with minimal staging and acting. In my reading I came across two examples of the use of Reader's Theatre in health professional education. The first described its use with nurses to enhance empathy, person centred care and reflection (Pardue, 2004). It concluded that

> Reader's Theatre provides students with the opportunity to explore empathetic connections and integrate reflection into their practice. (*Op.cit.*61)

The other described its use as a catalyst for discussion in a project to enhance interdisciplinary geriatric education (Macrae and Pardue, 2007). Of the Reader's Theatre experience, they say:

> Through the integration of this theatrical medium, students expressed a greater appreciation for the viewpoints of 'others', an enhanced ability to communicate and consider what 'the other' had to offer and, ultimately, they demonstrated the ability to design a comprehensive plan for client care. (*Op cit.*535).

Reader's Theatre has also been used as a means of data display and dissemination. Donmoyer and Yennie-Donmoyer (1995, 1998) suggest that Reader's Theatre as a presentational form of theatre is particularly useful for displaying research data. They suggest that minimisation of realism by holding and reading from scripts and by the use of stylisation in the staging encourages the audience member actively to construct meaning and engage with the issues presented.

I decided to construct a Reader's Theatre script from the data collected in the care co-ordination project, some time after the final report had been completed and accepted by the funders. As we worked with the data it became clear that the interview transcripts provided moving narrative accounts of parents' experiences of having a child with multiple disabilities and in some cases terminal illnesses, and their struggles to access the services their child needed. We had identified several themes in our early analysis that formed the basis of our findings. Much later, when I explored the data narratively rather than thematically, I came to see these themes as meta-narratives of a common struggle amongst this community to get the services needed for their child, against a backdrop of limited resources and interagency confusion. The care co-ordination schemes alleviated the struggle in a variety of ways but predominantly because parents saw the service as personal and flexible. There was a story to be told that wasn't adequately represented by our report, not because the report didn't say these things, but because it didn't quite reflect the humanity of what was provided nor the personal experience of the everyday lives of the parents who took part.

The research themes around which I organised the script were taken directly from the formal analysis and findings from the project. These can be summarised as:

- the difficulties experienced by parents and their need for emotional support
- parents fighting for scarce resources or services
- the positive impact of care co-ordination for most parents and key-workers
- the vulnerability and frustration felt by some key-workers.

In my first attempts at constructing dialogue from transcribed data I focused chiefly on these themes and went about it in much the same way as I would have chosen extracts of data which best exemplified the findings taken from the fully indexed data archive across all four schemes. In doing so I completely failed to produce anything that came close to credible dialogue or a coherent script. It took me some considerable time and an undergraduate module in scriptwriting to start to understand the nature of my failure. I had not managed to create believable characters through my amalgamation of data extracts and neither had I managed to create a sense of characters in dialogue with each other. In other words, my early efforts had shape through the playing out of research themes but that shape was not embodied or humanised in the way I had intended.

Reducing complexity

What followed was a daunting realisation that I needed to start again and re-conceptualise the task I had set myself. First, I decided to focus on parent data from only two of the schemes we had evaluated. Most of the parent data was collected from these two schemes, and they were also sufficiently similar in structure for extracts to be attributed to one imagined scheme. In my earlier attempts to represent all participants in all forms I had been thwarted by the cast of thousands that would be required. This time round I wanted to limit the number of characters to the minimum needed to portray the essential elements of our findings. By focusing on the two schemes that were most similar, I could use only one key-worker character, Kay Williams, through which to reveal the tensions, vulnerability and commitment that was evident in our data. I chose to represent the parents' experiences through three main parent characters, Mary, Susan and Pamela, each with a fictitious child and key worker. I intentionally made them all female characters as our parent participants had been almost exclusively women and the gendered nature of the narratives appeared to be significant.

Second, I considered the circumstances which could bring these four characters into discussion with each other, deciding on a reunion of people involved in the evaluation project at an event to celebrate the achievement of core funding for one of the schemes. The setting was intended to acknowledge the problem identified by the evaluation of properly resourcing the work of key workers and the range of services that parents said were so important to them. It also enabled me to introduce two further characters: Chris Cordis as the fictitious chair of the project steering group, whose dialogue would comprise extracts from policy documents and literature to place the schemes in the wider policy context and The Researcher, whose role was to turn the dialogue to the key themes in the findings. This role was the least successful when the script was performed. My reflections on my rather half-hearted attempt at providing this character with dialogue mirror my ambivalence about inserting a researcher's voice into the action. I will return to this issue in my reflections on the success of the script as a medium for disseminating research findings.

Creation of characters

In my second script, I recognised the need to create believable characters from the data. The simplest way to do this would be to construct characters around individual transcripts. In returning to the data I had already identified a number of narrative themes. For example, the theme of parents fighting for scarce resources or services could be seen as battle narratives and rescuing narratives that suggested inadequately implemented policy relating to multi-agency service provision that was ameliorated by the best efforts of key-workers. It would have been relatively easy to find an individual transcript for each character through which this and other narratives played out. We had, however, promised anonymity to our research participants and both the diagnosis of the child (sometimes of a very rare condition) and the personal nature of the stories told would have made the anonymity of individual accounts impossible.

So began a long and laborious process of bringing together several transcripts that were most likely to contribute to the construction of a single fictional character. My intention was to create from extracts across my selected transcripts, a kind of back-story for each character that could believably be read as a 'talking head' account of their experiences. Each transcript was initially reduced to the range of extracts that adequately reflected the essence of the individual account. From these extracted transcripts, I pieced together quotations that provided the narrative account of the fictitious character's experiences. Each character's story was therefore constructed almost entirely from verbatim data from more than one participant. The only insertions that were not from the data were small changes to improve the flow of the story. These changes were indicated with a different font and preserved in the script itself.

The tension between the real data and the fictionalised characters was a constant concern. This tension is exemplified in the following extract from the journal I kept while I was developing character back-stories:

> I've only managed a couple of sentences of back-story for each. There are problems in doing this. Firstly, each evocative sample of data *belongs* to that particular transcript – it has a relationship to other parts of the transcript. It is much more problematic to fragment an individual narrative than I'd first believed. For example, the extract I want to include about how a parent deals with the experience of knowing her child is going to die – (it's) important to

include because there is a thread across those stories from parents with terminally ill children that suggests it's not as bleak as we who haven't experienced those things imagine. If it were me I think I would cry every time I looked at my child. I wouldn't know how I could make one day follow the next – and yet in these transcripts parents talk about how they cope and how life isn't just one single awful wail. So the particular extract I want to use – about the hidden blessings a parent has found in looking after/loving a child who is going to die – is intricately connected to the individual and other things she has said. To take it away from the person who claims (not just to be a single mum[1]) would change the nature of her hidden blessings. What is significant is a whole mindset applied to a specific experience.

In the end I didn't use the extract above. The risk of revealing the parent's identity was too great and the meaning of the extract in isolation from the individual character of the parent would probably not have been characteristic of the fictitious parents I had created. Instead I used a different extract from the data that seemed a better fit with other utterances I had given to Mary, the fictitious mother of a terminally ill son, Jamie. I have Mary say:

> But as time's gone on you learn to live with it. I mean it's still in the back of your head but – how can I say? – you bury it and you get on with things, because it's the only thing you can do. I mean you could quite easily just sit and weep and wail, but that's no good to Jamie- he's got to have a life. We've got to make life as good for him for what time he's got so to just sit here and cry all day is helping nobody. So you just get on with things.

This tension between what is real and what is fictional in a script is a problem I will return to later when considering the extent to which the script is successful as a medium through which the findings from research can be portrayed and internalised.

In addition to amalgamating transcripts, I decided I would never include data that revealed the child's specific diagnosis. However I did include parent data that talked about their child's symptoms and the impact of diagnosis. These two versions of an extract from Susan's 'talking head' story shows how her description of her child's problems and his diagnosis have been taken from more than one transcript.

---

1. details omitted to preserve anonymity.

Version 1 (talking head)

Susan: There was something you couldn't put your finger on – there was just something about her and the colour of her didn't seem right – she sort of seemed a grey yellow sort of colour and the health visitor was coming in very regularly. He'd sit here with me for ages trying to give her a bottle and we couldn't get her to feed. She had terrible ear infections, horrendous sleep pattern, glue ear and couldn't – I had to sleep with her sitting up because every time she laid down she would scream in pain. It was the pressure building up. So we ended up through the hospital system. She had all sorts of tests and things and we then realised that there was something not quite right at all.

Version 2 (data extracts identified)

Parent 2: there was something you couldn't put your finger on – there was just something about her and the colour of her didn't seem right – she sort of seemed a grey yellow sort of colour and the health visitor was coming in very regularly he'd sit here with me for ages trying to give her a bottle and we couldn't get her to feed.

Parent 4: she had terrible ear infections, horrendous sleep pattern, glue ear and couldn't – I had to sleep with her sitting up because every time she laid down she would scream in pain, it was the pressure building up so we ended up through the hospital system.

Parent 2: she had all sorts of tests and things and we then realised that there was something not quite right at all

I would select the dialogue for the script from these individual stories. In the following extract two parents and the key worker are discussing experiences of having their children diagnosed:

Susan: *She had terrible ear infections, horrendous sleep pattern, glue-ear and couldn't – I had to sleep with her sitting up because every time she laid down she would scream in pain. It was the pressure building up. So we ended up through the hospital system and she had all sorts of tests and things and we then realised that there was something not quite right at all.*

> *Kay Williams: In my experience, it probably has been explained to parents lots and lots of times, but they have so much going on all the time that it doesn't sink in. That's the biggest difficulty.*
>
> *Mary: Well I just went numb, completely numb, and I had to get the doctor to – to put it all on to paper and all the words – all the big words. I weren't really told half of what I know now – no – what I've taught myself...*

At first, the selection of transcripts for each character was based mainly on similarity of the narrative across transcripts but other factors such as use of language and voice also became important as I engaged with each developing character. For example, as I came to piece together each back-story, it was clear that the way some participants expressed things was so unlike others, that the data couldn't credibly belong to the same character even if the narrative accounts were similar. So I had to let go of favoured sets of transcripts in terms of content for those where utterances could credibly be linked together in the same character.

In selecting transcripts to amalgamate I had already formed an idea of the number and kind of characters I needed to reflect the research themes and the range of difficulties which parents faced. For example, although the findings of the evaluation were overwhelmingly positive, one or two parents voiced dissatisfaction. It would have been an over-representation to make one of the three characters entirely dissatisfied and so I decided to create a character, Pamela, who had reservations and presented a slightly darker tone to her view of the keyworker scheme. When, towards the end, parents are talking about how the service affected their lives Pamela says:

> *I felt initially good about it, I really felt that here were these people who were doing this special thing that was going to help us out, and then sometimes I listened to the advice and I thought 'oh I'm not really sure about that one' – so I didn't always think that the advice they gave us was appropriate, be-cause they didn't know us well enough and they didn't know Ben well enough, and they didn't actually know, because I suppose they hadn't got to know us and knew what we were all about ...I think it's probably improved more now because ... its just coordinating and trying to get everybody to-gether and think along the same lines, and what's best for Ben educationally.*

My characters and setting decided upon, I then returned to the research themes to provide momentum and shape to the dialogue I was about to create. The draft outline I created for the script included the following themes:

- reacting to the child's diagnosis and symptoms
- what life was like before the care co-ordination scheme
- the impact of the child's difficulties on the rest of the family
- the difficulty of managing the number of different professionals involved in the child's care
- the need for emotional support
- the financial consequences of looking after a child with such complex needs
- the need to fight for scarce resources
- the burden of bureaucracy when trying to access services or resources
- the impact of being allocated a key worker
- what key workers do to help
- what if the scheme ended?

Finally, because I wanted to use the script in the classroom with health professional students, I decided that the script should be performed in about thirty minutes so that there would be sufficient time for students to discuss and debate the issues raised and reflect on the implications for practice.

Discussion

As a medium for data display the script had some clear advantages over the formal report we had written. In presenting data as fictitious dialogue I could portray triangulation between participant groups in ways not available to me in writing a full report. For example, when compared, the data from parents and the data from key workers showed that there was a difference in perception about how well the role was functioning. Key workers often expressed uncertainty about how they were interpreting their role and their ability to manage the complexity of the multi-professional, multi-agency relationships through which services for the child were delivered. The majority of parents, on the other hand, claimed that key workers had considerably helped manage the complexity of those services and had released parents from the burden of multiple communications. I was able to show this difference by juxtaposing the two perceptions in the dialogue between the key worker and Pamela.

> Pamela: *I kind of see them as pulling everything together – being there to sort of, not take control, because I do see that as my job, controlling Ben's environment and stuff, but just being there to oversee if you like, the whole sort of structure of how Ben gets on at school, and how he gets on health wise, social wise, everything else – just like a big net pulling everything in together, and holding everything together, and supporting the whole thing.*

> Kay Williams: *I often feel that I'm not quite pulling it all together and I feel that might be a lack of skill on my behalf – if there was more concrete guidance I think that would be, the key working role being so open ended and so open to interpretation – its very difficult to know what to do ... I feel that I'm not quite pulling it all together for the family as a whole. But the families know that I'm available and I'm there to help them. They're not on their own – there is somebody else out there for them.*

A key question relates to the extent to which a fictitious scripted dialogue, albeit using verbatim data, can be said to represent the reality of experience. Although I had made a serious attempt at representing the findings from the systematic analysis of the evaluation data fairly, the final version of the script was one of many that I could have produced. It had been a creative act to put together the words of participants in the form that I chose. Clearly some elements of the script were fictional. The characters as I represented them were not to be found amongst the research participants and neither were the off-stage people they referred to in their dialogue. Therefore how well does such an endeavour succeed as an instrument for disseminating research findings and, in relation to my particular aspiration, as a medium for students to engage with research data in the classroom?

When compared with our formal evaluation report it is clear that both have been constructed and neither can claim to represent reality independently from the choices and interpretation of researchers. This idea is not new. In discussing the constructed nature of writing social science Laurel Richardson says:

No textual staging is innocent. We are always inscribing values in our writing. It is unavoidable. ... No matter how we stage the text, we – as authors – are doing the staging. As we speak about the people we study, we also speak for them. As we inscribe their lives, we bestow meaning and promulgate values. (Richardson, 1990:12)

In comparing it to scientific writing she goes on to say:

But we should not be fooled. Science writing, like all other forms of writing, is a sociohistorical construction that is narratively driven and depends upon literary devices not just for adornment but for cognitive meaning. (*Op cit.*13)

In staging the text given to me by participants as a script for performance and inscribing it with my own values and priorities, I was concerned that the script would not be recognisable to those people whose experience it was meant to represent. Irrationally (according to what Richardson suggests above) I didn't have the same concerns about the evaluation report. I therefore wanted to return to participant groups to see what they thought of the way in which I had constructed their experiences in the script. I met with the person who had led the group who had funded the evaluation and with the key informants from the two schemes I had used. I gave them the script and talked about what I had done. The response from them was positive and enthusiastic. They also helped provide access to the community of parents from which participants had been recruited. The way in which we had anonymised transcripts before indexing and archiving meant that a return to individual parent participants would not be possible. Instead, I sought the views of a well-subscribed parent group, set up and run by parents of children with complex needs. It was likely that many of their members had taken part in our evaluation, so some may well have contributed to the data used in the script. To illustrate what I had done I sent them a copy of the script, filmed a reading of it and made a DVD to show them extracts of how the research themes would be revealed and experienced in the classroom. The members I met disseminated the script to all their members and invited comments. Their response was overwhelmingly positive and encouraging. The secretary summarised their responses as follows:

The responses from (*name of group*) about the Encounters script are all positive. Comments such as it 'seems to capture some of the frustrations and difficulties' and 'a fairly balanced piece of work' were common. There was also a comment from a parent of a child on the life limited/palliative care side which said 'realistic and non-judgemental'. The question of paperwork around terminally ill was raised and those able to comment said it was correct and could relate to it. All in all this gets the thumbs up from (*name of group*). May we wish you well with this very important and appropriate piece of work'(email correspondence 4/02/08).

The reference above to 'paperwork around terminally ill' relates to a specific worry I had about the script and its authenticity. One of the major research themes centred on the burden of bureaucracy which parents found especially difficult before they had the support of a key worker. In the script I therefore had Mary say:

> *They are like a minefield those forms. They don't actually say in them but, its like wording everything correctly so that you're not lying, but so that you're painting it in the right picture for people to understand when they read a form – 'cos they are only little boxes you have to fill in – and wording everything right, when you are writing things down about your sick child, is the most horrendous thing in the world, 'cos you have to read it back to make sure you've done it right, and you end up just being in floods of tears – and I must admit to – me I couldn't understand, and I still don't understand, why I have to do it every six months 'cos I found it exhausting, and it usually took me about a week to do it, even with the help of one of the nurses...they are complicated, and I know, I understand and appreciate they have to be done correctly – but I don't understand why on earth, when a child's got a diagnosis for something which they ain't going to get rid of, why they can't just review it with the paediatrician or something, just ask for the letter to say that 'yes they still are in this condition'.*

Later, when colleagues read the script for the first time, one of them said that they didn't think a parent with a terminally ill child would have to fill in forms regularly. I had pieced together this utterance from two parents, one of whom had a terminally ill child and the other whose child had a condition which would not improve but she might not necessarily die. I wanted to check out with the parent group whether Mary's words rang true with those whose circumstances were similar to Mary's. The members I met agreed to pursue it further but suggested that this might be a common perception of parents even though there might have been a reduction in paperwork if a child was diagnosed with a long-term condition or was terminally ill. What was interesting about this exchange was that it exemplified the different versions of reality and truth that were held by health professionals and parents. Form filling may have been dramatically curtailed for parents in this position, but how parents experienced any request for information about their sick child was so emotionally powerful and draining that it was a serious burden. As Mary says a little later in the script:

Yeah – guts me every time I have to do it, to be perfectly honest with you.

Had I been adventurous enough not to rely on the data so exclusively, I believe the script would have benefited from some fictitious dialogue about this contested view of form-filling. However, at the time I felt constrained because I had no data from health professionals through which to reflect their different perceptions.

A major aim of using Reader's Theatre in the classroom had been to encourage students to engage with data in ways that they probably would not engage with formal research papers and reports. I wanted to humanise the issues raised by the research so that experiences could be contextualised and personalised. In doing so I believed that the lessons that could be taken into students' practice would be more powerful and memorable. Even with these intentions I was not prepared for the reaction of a group of research students the first time I ran it as a workshop on representing data. This particular group of students came from a variety of professions, all within some form of human services. Having set the context of the research the group performed the script. During the reading two students became upset and had to leave the room for a short while. Afterwards, we explored the emotional impact of the script.

Members of the group described the way in which the embodied data in the script forced an identification with the characters which data extracts in reports were less likely to do. For those members of the group who had young children of their own the emotional response to such identification was too much to control. My first reaction was to feel guilty and I wanted to hurry away and remove the most emotionally challenging dialogue from the script. I was discouraged from doing this by my colleagues and the students themselves. They challenged the presumption that an intense emotional response was the wrong response. The success of the care co-ordination schemes was in part attributable to the ability of the key worker to empathise with parents' experiences and offer emotional as well as practical help. As Susan says of her key worker towards the end of the script:

> But there are a few people who go beyond what's expected of them, who move beyond their professional job description and who really, truly, personally know that when you are struggling for something, you really are – and they can't leave you, cos they really know that – but they know that because they know you personally I think.

How do health professionals learn to empathise with the experiences of others? How do they learn not to deny their own emotional responses nor guard against them by inappropriate distancing strategies? If parents particularly value services that they experience as personal and relevant to their everyday struggles, then perhaps in the classroom students should be given opportunities to engage their humanity and identify with human experience in a personal and embodied way.

I want to consider the incorporation of the researcher's voice in the script. Earlier I suggested that my failure to create a believable character for The Researcher showed my general ambivalence about whether it was right to give the researcher a voice. In doing so, was I not allowing the data from participants to speak for itself? Did I not trust the reader or audience to come to the right conclusions? Could I not resist the opportunity to lead the audience to find what we had found from the data and use my own inserted rhetoric to exert control, which Richardson claims is 'not ornamental but instrumental in the 'persuasive discourse' of science' (Richardson, 1990:15)? On the other hand, would omitting the voice of the researcher be a contrivance? The data from which the dialogue is drawn did not exist in isolation from the researcher who collected them. Parents told their stories to a researcher in the context of a research project. If there were no researcher role in the script, would I have been guilty of obscuring the co-constructed nature of the data and my authorship like the scientist who writes of their work in the third person to create an illusion of objectivity?

In the end, I decided that the researcher role should stay, but it remains an unresolved dilemma. Although I continue to feel uncomfortable with that decision, its inclusion has already facilitated interesting debate with students about researcher voice and control.

At the close of this chapter, looking back over the things I have written, I am aware of the distance I've travelled since I first had the idea of writing a Reader's Theatre script. One of the most important differences between then and now lies in how I view the practice of research and how much wider I draw the boundaries of any single research enterprise. My sense of what constitutes dissemination has been transformed from a narrow listing of potential outputs for a variety of stakeholder, to a much broader and potentially more exciting sense of getting those audiences to engage fully with the human experience to which research findings often refer. An important audience for research about health services and practice is the body of students who are preparing to become the next generation of health professionals: early responses to this project suggest that it's an effective way of engaging students with research data.

With hindsight, I can see a number of things I would do differently. I would not be as fearful of fictionalising more of the script, particularly where verbatim data alone could not adequately portray an important interpretation of the data. I would pay more attention to the credibility of all the characters. For example, if I had developed a fictitious backstory for The Researcher' the role would probably have been more believable in the script and I could have used it more effectively to demonstrate the co-constructed nature of the data. I would also try to make the finished product more consistently readable rather than slavishly adhere to the sometimes faltering utterances of the verbatim data.

For others who may wish to try their hand at ethnodrama this is my advice:

- Try and team up with someone who has scriptwriting expertise. It will probably save you a great deal of time.
- Have a clear sense of the shape of the story you want to portray before you start.
- Keep it simple with a manageable cast of characters.
- Create rounded and believable characters.
- Don't get overly attached to specific sections of data.
- Get colleagues to read and comment on an early draft and be prepared to change it.

Above all, I recommend it as an exciting and fulfilling experience. It can generate additional theoretical insights by re-presenting the data in markedly different forms.

8

A DAY IN DECEMBER

Linden Wilkinson

Introduction

This is a case study of the development of my verbatim theatre play, *A Day in December*, from performed research for my master's degree to a full theatrical production. The script is about a railway accident and its impact on a small outer urban community.

During this process of changing demands and expectations the script evolved through three distinct phases in terms of length, content and structure. Called *Remembering Glenbrook* for a static performed reading at the outset, its title changed to *Remembering a Day in December* as having potentially greater appeal to an audience which was broader than the community that first initiated the research data. It then went into rehearsal for a stage production, during which the content was re-shaped again to accentuate its emerging themes of trauma and resilience. Before it opened its title changed for the third time to *A Day in December*.

Thus did *Remembering Glenbrook* become *A Day in December*. Despite the challenges of the form, especially for stage, it remains a verbatim theatre play and I believe the interest it has generated can be directly attributed to the authentic voice of its content. My research journey to locate the content began after a chance conversation in 2006, but the play's story really starts in 1999.

The inciting event

On a fine, clear morning at 8.22am on December 2, 1999, a four car fibreglass inter-urban commuter train crashed into the rear of the Indian Pacific, a long and heavy train. The collision occurred on the bends in the track just past Glenbrook railway station in outer Sydney's Blue Mountains. Seven people travelling in the first carriage of the inter-urban were killed instantly; the steel car-carrying carriage at the rear of the Indian Pacific sliced through the front mezzanine 'like a tin-opener, it was just like psschooo!' The driver of the inter-urban escaped serious injury as he ran back into the carriage yelling a warning, when he knew a crash was imminent. The statistics show that 51 people were injured in the crash and that there were no entrapments. It was a quick and commendable rescue operation. But the statistics, as the play reveals, do not tell the only true story.

In 2006 a conversation with a close friend revealed that she felt her partner hadn't really been the same 'since Glenbrook'. I knew she was referring to the rail disaster and that he had been on that train. I didn't know that he had been in the first carriage nor did I understand the significance of that at the time. Surprised, I asked why Glenbrook had had such an impact. Statistically it was minor in comparison to the monumental Granville train disaster 22 years before, which also involved a Blue Mountains commuter train. My friend replied that she didn't know why her partner had been affected by Glenbrook; he wouldn't talk about it.

The Granville train disaster remains Australia's worst rail accident: 83 commuters were killed and 213 were injured when an early morning commuter train from the Blue Mountains derailed just after Granville station and slammed into the pylons of an overhead road bridge, causing the concrete slabs of the bridge to collapse on to the third and fourth carriages of the derailed train. Granville's impact dwarfed that of Glenbrook in terms of scale but it affected exactly the same population. Interviews revealed that Granville still casts long shadows; the Glenbrook survivors, who came forward to tell me their stories, acknowledged that Granville contributed to their reticence to talk about Glenbrook. Often participants said that they had never told anyone what they were now telling me; that they had tried to dismiss the event because they felt no-one wanted to hear what they had to say. My friend's partner was not alone in choosing to be silent.

The research project

Having immersed myself in what I believe is a resurgence of the verbatim theatre form, I knew when I began my research that I wanted to write a verbatim play. I decided to investigate the Glenbrook rail disaster because I felt there might be something to solve, something to understand; my friend's partner's silence intrigued me. I had lived at Glenbrook and was familiar with the Blue Mountains experience of community. It's rugged, spectacular country with small urban townships fringing a vast National Park. As bushfires are a constant threat, living there is a conscious choice and the implicit presence of physical danger heightens a sense of inter-dependency and fraternity.

I advertised in the Blue Mountains Gazette for participants; six people responded. I invited two others, who had been on 'that train' to contribute. I also included my friend, who hadn't been on the train, and her partner. They became Lisa and Stu in the play, and all the names of the characters are pseudonyms of the original informants. Lisa and Stu took my research pool to a total of ten participants. I expected to need many more and hoped to rely on passive snowballing, as well as my own contacts to boost numbers. However I found the stories of those that came forward so gripping I looked no further.

In the light of the play's development, as a researcher I regret this decision. The participants that came forward were all adults at the time of the crash; the two that I invited to contribute were still at school in 1999 but were in the third carriage. In hindsight I would like to have included the language and the experiences of a school-age individual or group who were in the first carriage. None came forward at the time and I didn't persist in my investigative efforts in the field. This was partly because of the strength of the stories I had located and partly because I found that the outcomes from passive snowballing were disappointing. I discovered that if participants hadn't come forward voluntarily, they didn't have a story to tell. Their narratives were no more than an interview, whose content had been dictated by my questions.

The notion that the story will emerge from the data is inherent in both verbatim theatre (Paget, 1987) and most ethnodrama forms. This was confirmed by a colleague, Ros Horin, in an interview on her process for *Through the Wire* (2004), her verbatim play about detainees: 'I didn't start with a concept of how I was going to put it together. I thought: I will let the material reveal itself to me' (2005).

As the participants in my project were now talking about an event that occurred six years before, all of them dwelt on their difficulty of dealing with its aftermath. Their narratives, poignant and emotional, spoke of a deep courage that they had located after experiencing profound disillusionment. Nothing in their lives before this had prepared them for long-term trauma. What they thought would bring closure, immediate counselling and the Public Inquiry into the train accident, not only failed to deliver comfort, but exacerbated their anger and sense of isolation. To tell their stories as a play I knew I would have to trust the verbatim theatre form and include documentary material from the world beyond their own narratives, especially the Public Inquiry (2000). It was not an easy decision to include extracts from the Public Inquiry in *Remembering Glenbrook*, but the story that was emerging from the field data could not be told without it. Like media reports of the accident, the Public Inquiry compartmentalised the event. It analysed the events that led to the collision, made recommendations to the then State Rail Authority, reached its conclusions and figuratively moved on. This was exactly what the participants couldn't do. The Inquiry revealed conflict between individuals and the State: a conflict of expectations, of responsibilities, a conflict between cultures. And as the truism goes, 'conflict is at the heart of all drama'.

Transcripts from the ten participant narratives were collapsed into dialogue for eight characters by a process of rigorous editing. As my intention had always been to write a verbatim play, when I collected data from the field I was attuned not only to what was said but how. Recorded interviews became unedited verbatim transcripts, with each nuance of language and every emotional colouration included as far as possible. Hesitations, repetitions, laughter and tears all became clues for actors in performance, helping them to create distinct but always accessible and authentic voices.

The edited transcripts and extracts from the Public Inquiry were inter-woven to become the first draft of the play. *Remembering Glenbrook* was read by a core group of eight experienced actors for a small group of invited family, friends and research participants in Penrith, only minutes away from Glenbrook, in 2007. It was approximately 83 minutes in length; it had no interval and was well received. This parti-cular draft would go on to have three more public readings with dif-ferent actors and the audience response each time was encouraging, with one exception.

The play was nothing like I expected it to be. Denzin (2003) defines the exploration of community crises and subsequent moments of cultural epiphany as the essence of Performance Ethnography. I had chosen a rail disaster specifically because I knew it would yield material suitable for dramatisation; people died, people were in peril, people escaped. My experience as a professional writer taught me that the scenario was rich in crisis potential. However, where I expected the drama to be was not where I found it and that was very disconcerting.

Prior learning and the lure of the three act structure

I thought I would spend most of my play in the first carriage of the com-muter train. This carriage sustained the most damage and was where the deaths occurred. Having been a professional script writer and per-former for thirty years, my craft knowledge told me that this would be where I would locate the classic disaster format scenario. Implicit in this assumption is the idea that the three act disaster would be the only story that would emerge from the accident. As Aronson (2000) explains, the disaster formula involves a three act structure, which deals with a group under threat and is a vehicle for one heroic figure to be seen as triumphant against the odds. So as I headed up the mountains, as a fledgling researcher, I was instinctively looking for a couple of options: the one, where multiple victims are eventually freed from the carriage due to the heroic leadership of one of them or, alternatively, when all hope has gone, someone manages to bring a survivor out alive. I knew that either scenario would have been good for television: the main action contained in the carriage and in the dénouement the survivors all go home; some grieving their losses and others counting their bless-ings. But, as Bowles points out, representation in the media is the end point of a series of production choices; it has 'some kind of relationship to something else we call reality' (2006:64). I discovered quickly that what I was uncovering in the field was not a media story; it was something else and I was in unfamiliar territory.

Although the collision figured prominently as the participants began their narratives, once it was out of the way they didn't return to it. Furthermore there were no entrapments. Victims weren't left languishing in the carriage; passengers either died or were removed in under an hour. The speed of the recovery operation was a distinguishing feature of the Glenbrook Rail Disaster. As a screen writer, I found myself short of material. As a researcher I discovered that the real drama was in the aftermath, the years that followed the collision.

In hearing the participants' stories of anger, endurance, resilience and discovery I experienced the intense relational shift inherent in narrative inquiry, as observed by Clandinin and Connelly (2000). I was now aware that there would be a conflict between my experiences as an early researcher and my years of accumulating theatre-craft and knowledge. When I came to selecting content from the transcripts, I knew that I would need to question whether what I intuited was good material was also true to the research. And I knew my play would not fit into a comfortable format box.

Remembering Glenbrook – the structure

The overall finding in the narratives was that the experience of the rail disaster was isolating. Unlike *Aftershocks* (Brown *et al*, 1993) or *Through the Wire* (Horin, 2004) the participants did not know each other, nor did the accident bring them together. Because there were no entrapments, there were no displays of heroism in the *Aftershocks* sense. Because the participants were not on either side of a dysfunctional law, as in *Through the Wire*, their narratives didn't lead to empathic and cathartic understandings of each other.

The stories that are relived and retold in *Remembering Glenbrook* are about suffering and struggling alone and the consequences of that struggle. Heroism is more subtly located; it's in the participants' refusal to obliterate the experience from memory; in their efforts to grow by facing their overwhelming sense of vulnerability; and in their loss of innocence, because of their proximity to sudden death.

So the challenge was to try to find a way to translate this lonely but heroic journey, which had to be told by multiple voices, into compelling drama. The play's structure had to create a dramatic unity, the transcripts' content did not. The material had to allow opportunities for characters to share their experiences so that the play could move forwards with a collective momentum. Relationships that did not exist in the field had to be created in performance.

Not all of the participants were on the train. Of those that were: Stu, Chris, Dan, Susan, Rita and Mitch, only the first four were in the first carriage; Rita and Mitch were further back in the train and didn't know how bad it was for some passengers until they were walking up the track towards Glenbrook station. Lisa, Stu's partner, was on her way to work; Police Rescue Officer Dave had just clocked on for the day further up the line at Springwood and Cityrail employee Martin was travelling to work in the train behind. Josie lived in Glenbrook and heard the crash; her testimony eventually became incorporated in Lisa's and in Dan's. In *Remembering Glenbrook*, Mitch and Martin could be played by the same actor, because their characters were active in different sections of the play.

The perspectives that, particularly Dave, as a Rescue Policeman, and Martin, as a railway worker, contributed to the overall story were invaluable; so I had to find a structure that could incorporate everyone's transcript content. When it came to editing the transcripts, I looked for common threads in the narratives. I divided the material into five chapters:

Living there – about the Blue Mountains
My God, we're running into the back of that train – the journey towards impact
The Signals – the causes of the disaster
Carnage – inside the train
Aftermath – dealing with the trauma

Living there was about community; it struck a light note and allowed the characters to establish themselves. *My God, we're running into the back of that train* was about being on that particular train that particular morning; the passenger/participants talked about the actions of the train driver and most of them mentioned watching a playful six year-old boy with a Mohawk and his mother. Both of these passengers died in the collision and worse, were visible in the wreckage. Material for *The Signals* came from the Public Inquiry; *Carnage* begins just after collision; *Aftermath* begins the next day and ends in the present.

This structure was observed in the performed readings; the chapter titles were read by the character who had the first lines of dialogue. This was a particularly useful convention, when there were no other effects to create a change of scene. In terms of content, the bulk of the data was in chapters four and five: *Carnage* and *Aftermath*.

Remembering Glenbrook – the content

Once I had separated the content into chapters, I began searching through the transcripts for data links either in terms of consecutive moments in time or conflicting reports of the same event. I was attempting to layer the content with multiple experiences of the truth; the more these experiences differed, the more dramatic tension would be created in performance, as each character sought to be heard. By utilising recurring narrative threads, I was able to organise testimonies into blocks of dialogue. By being aware of the content's chronology, I hoped to create dramatic momentum.

At this crucial stage of data selection I was again strongly influenced by the findings of a local practitioner. Kate Gaul has had a long career in verbatim theatre and directed the Sydney production of *The Laramie Project* (Kaufman, 2001) for Belvoir's Company B at Belvoir Theatre in 2001.

> The thing I have learnt about verbatim theatre is that you need a good crisis and a dramatic clock. Marginalised groups are in crisis and it is a crisis where you can say well that's right and that's wrong and we need to get social justice for this. You should be able to make a play out of anything if the tension is there. Somehow the theatre won't let you get away without either of those things not being present. Something's gone wrong and the clock ticks and there is a problem that has to be solved. Without that the play just meanders and people get bored and it never comes off. (2005)

The idea of a ticking clock was easier to locate in the script prior to the accident, as the inter-urban hurtled towards the Indian Pacific. Several passengers among my participants distinctly remembered the driver running through the train:

Chris:	I was sort of asleep and you heard the door bang – like it was a really loud sort of bang....that was apparently the driver running back through the train.... and he said, he just said: Hold On, Look Out, you know, something like that, shouted it, you know, kind of really loud.
Susan:	We heard somebody shout: Hold On or Hang on! We're going to crash! And then a thump and that thump was him jumping down the three or four stairs to go down to the lower part of the carriage.
Martin:	He sang out as he ran through the carriage, Run! Run! Get to the back of the carriage! There's going to be a train crash!
Dan:	He actually ran past the little kid and he yelled, I'm sure he yelled: Get out or something. But he could have grabbed that little kid and just tossed him down the stairs or something.
Rita:	We were told everybody thought he was mad.
Martin:	'Cos um he would have been filled with fear and running through the carriage himself. Oh, is this a crazy person or what?
Rita:	He'd come through screaming, you know, Crash position! Crash position! It probably wouldn't have helped those poor souls.

The experience of the crash itself created tension, not through urgency but through the characters' slow recall of the horror of what had happened. The speeches below are extracts from those in the play and are shortened to emphasise the layering effect of juxtaposing testimony.

| Mitch: | I guess I mainly remember the noise... like really, really tearing, painful metallic noise, like a lawnmower running over rocks or something... |

Dan, Stu and Rita then describe their experiences of the train tilting, while travelling at speed. But Chris's subsequent memory of the collision propels the play into the deep trauma of witnessing sudden death.

| Chris: | ....it was like Godzilla had picked up the train, shook it, then threw it on the ground. Um... and ah... yeah, there was this black thing in the stairwell and I just couldn't figure out what it was ... what the hell is that?... and then it kind of dawned on me. Well this is kind of like... bad... So there was this black |

thing in the stairwell... it was this metal black thing in the
stairwell... and ah (begins to cry) it was the Indian Pacific. Yeah.
Squished everyone. Yeah. there was ah... breathing) ... (begins
to cry) Shouldn't be upset about it ... I didn't expect to be – to
be upset. (Laughs with unease) There you go. Cool ... So I
went through the train and then got out of the train ... and I was
actually the first person to go up to the window ...

In Dan's following speech he remembers seeing people thrown about the carriage but he can't remember hearing anything. He mentions seeing one of the deceased but he doesn't explore that memory with Chris's detail. Juxtaposing their two experiences allowed the play to move forward, just as the participants had to on the day itself.

Chris: *... this window... was ... it was just like full of all the stuff and like*
people ... there was two ... remembered there was two people,
obviously – obviously dead that I could see sitting in the
window of the train ... and it was awful ... it looked like a
garbage compactor, you know ... like sort of like the back of a
garbage truck. It looked like that, just with people in it, you
know, it was just horrific ...

Dan: *... I don't want to talk about that anymore. Yeah.*

But the heart of the play was not in the collision but in the participants' reflection of its residual impact. In *Aftermath* the participants struggle to come to terms with trauma over time and, although this was passive, the content in the performed readings remained engaging for the actors and audience alike. However, *Aftermath* could not be fully appreciated unless the play included investigative extracts from the complicated, technical Public Inquiry. Such extracts would possibly alienate audiences and put their receptivity towards the whole play at risk.

The signals – the problematic chapter three

The inclusion of extracts from the first Glenbrook Inquiry is a leap of faith. It reflects my interest in and experiential understanding of Arnold's work on Empathic Intelligence (2005). Receptivity, Arnold claims, is enhanced by having both emotional and intellectual content. Chapter three tells the collision story; it gives a detailed account of all the factors that contributed to the disaster. In terms of the dramatic narrative it gets the technical details out of the way, so the rest of the text can focus on the core of the play: what happened to the people involved. But it is a complete departure in dramatic style. However, because the Inquiry also includes the railway workers' dialogue, it gives the actors an opportunity to create other characters. These quick exchanges, crucial for establishing evidence of relaxed safety standards, contribute to the stylistic shift and go some way to counter-acting the weight of the technical findings. The railway workers' language contrasts with the precise scientific, investigative language of the court and the emotional unfinished sentences of the passengers. Conscious that I was choosing to make a radical departure in this chapter, I introduced the Justice character as an archetypal authority figure in chapter two as a way of introducing another kind of voice, which prepared the way for both Martin and Dave, who have more objectivity in their narratives than the other participants.

But overall the content of the chapter is difficult to follow. The two trains were meant to be eleven minutes apart; how they came to collide is a confusion of broken signals, poor communication and human error. For an audience the play text here is hard to navigate. But after the performed readings of *Remembering Glenbrook* audience feedback suggested that although this chapter was confusing, the content was engrossing and informative. In facing the challenge of taking the material to the stage for *A Day in December*, I hoped the content could be simplified with the use of visual prompts: slides perhaps or graphs. Unfortunately the budget wouldn't stretch that far and the chapter remained dialogue-dependent.

Although the text has now been heavily pruned, I don't believe I could cut it out altogether and still maintain the integrity of the play. The chapter contains a lot of Martin's valuable testimony about New South Wales railways and train operations. It also carries the essence of the participants' inner conflict discussed earlier, between what they expected and what they felt. The detached legal language also contrasted with that in the remaining two chapters, *Carnage* and *Aftermath* and the summation on the Inquiry created a wonderfully understated beginning to the remainder of the play.

> Justice: At 8.22 and 18 seconds the inter-urban train W534 slammed
> into the motorail at the rear of the Indian Pacific. Given the

*reduced separation time, the slow speed of the Indian Pacific,
its position in the cutting and the speed at which the inter-
urban train proceeded from Glenbrook railway station towards
the cutting, a collision of some violence was inevitable.*

Because it ignores the human toll of the collision, we can share in the participants' disillusionment with the legal system. Figuratively the case is dismissed, the book is closed and the participants' nightmares continue.

But chapter three is only one of the departures from a conventional dramatic structure. The other is *Aftermath*, the final chapter. The narratives here reveal the most compelling research but they do not deliver a climax.

Finding the final turning point

There is no one event in *Aftermath* which resolves the central dilemma of the *Remembering Glenbrook* story. Rita expresses this dilemma as:

Rita: *Why can't people pick up themselves, wipe their shoes and
get on with their lives and that's it! You don't sit and dwell on
things! I just feel trauma is a strange thing, you don't know
about it until you actually experience it.*

The play has multiple protagonists, who not only do not know each other but are also further isolated by the inciting event, the train accident. But all the participants in *Aftermath* have a catharsis, in which the audience can simultaneously share. This catharsis is not one of an 'emotional unravelling' (Mienczakowski *et al*, 2002:42), as *un*ravelling is the participants' starting point in the beginning of the play.

In *Aftermath* most of the characters express new understandings of the healing process and their insights invigorate them with a sense of hope and a new wholeness. Dan is able to think about other things; Lisa learned to be kind and tells us that Stu eventually got a little bit of momentum; Susan knows the human spirit is very strong; Dave knows people can dig deep; Rita learned that wonderful lesson, compassion; Chris has learned to accept it as part of the mix of his life. But none of them feel good about it; none of them can say: 'Looking back I feel grateful' Or 'I achieved closure'. And I found this journey towards acceptance inspirational; it's a story I hadn't heard before.

By the end of the play the characters know that healing isn't getting over something; healing is about expanding the many facets of themselves to incorporate trauma, to try and balance it. Healing is about being more in life, rather than less, and that's the difficulty. I didn't know whether an audience would respond similarly, but to me, this realisation was profound. As a playwright I would like to have been able to make sure it was clear, maybe add some dialogue, lay it on with a trowel, as they say. As a researcher I had to trust that some aspect of this idea would be there without any help – and if it wasn't, perhaps it was destined to be my personal discovery from living with and learning from the data.

That the play had a transformative aspect, where the characters' catharsis generated an empathic response in an audience, emerged as a possibility when *Remembering Glenbrook* had its first reading in Penrith, just near Glenbrook, in 2007. With the help of a local Blue Mountains theatre group, Weatherboard, a cast of eight professional actors gathered to rehearse, prior to the reading. In discussing the play afterwards the cast suggested that the play had universal themes; that it was about more than a train accident, it was also about the complexity of trauma and the nature of resilience. It was a story for everyone. On hearing feedback like this, *Aftermath* justified itself; it was long, but it was crucial and perhaps an audience's engagement outweighed the need for a conventional climax.

Four of the research participants attended the first public reading of *Remembering Glenbrook* and reinforced this new understanding of the play's resonance. They all commented after the reading that they had enjoyed the reading, because they never knew anyone else had felt the same as they had. Attending the performance had been restorative; it reaffirmed not just their journey but their humanity.

But not all the readings met with such a positive response.

A confrontation

Remembering Glenbrook had its third reading in August, 2007. The reading was attended by a number of friends, theatre practitioners and members of the public. It was also attended by a close relative of two of the deceased. She did not stay for the discussion after the performance but shared her responses by email the following week.

She had major concerns with the play: there was no warning that the play's content would be so shocking; in one of Dan's stories I had exposed a living member of her family without his permission and the play offered no de-brief. She also intimated that Dave's speech about finding the bodies in the first carriage was exploitative and sensationalist. Immediately I felt two disparate and simultaneous emotional responses to her criticisms: deep regret that the play had troubled her and a feisty determination not to self-censor the participants' memories.

On a practical level I made some decisions. I included a warning to be read at the beginning of the play saying that some people might find the content disturbing; I blurred the identity of her family member and for peace of mind had the play read by a defamation lawyer, who made several other small recommendations, which I implemented. I shelved the idea of a de-brief, deciding it was implicit in the current draft. But I did have to consider whether I had deliberately included sensationalist material.

During the interview process I had asked Dave to be more explicit about the state of the bodies. He elaborated with details we would take for granted in a television action drama. But as a researcher I chose to restrict Dave's description to the state of the bodies and how it affected him and his crew. Dave dealt with massive injuries and death as part of his job; his language was no nonsense, factual and contrasted sharply with that used by the passenger participants. His contribution enriched the text and deepened an audience's understanding of the event. It had to be there.

Ultimately I decided that my intention had always been to inform, not to sensationalise nor exploit. What happened in that carriage was what the participants had wanted to share in the data gathering process. Although I felt sorry for this particular audience member, I elected not to edit the text to accommodate her.

Ironically her reaction illuminated the community attitudes the participants had found most difficult to live with: that because they were walking, they were well, that no-one wanted to hear, no-one wanted to know what they had been through, what they had witnessed. Although, like them, I felt condemned for my story, I chose to share what Arnold

(2005) refers to as the 'psychic landscape' of the participants and to take responsibility for that outcome.

Though I never imagined it would be at the time, the issue of a de-brief proved to be an invaluable suggestion. The play was already running at 83 minutes. The last thing it needed, I thought, was more material. However, when the play was given the chance of a production, this is exactly what was required.

The NIDA Short Course Program

The National Institute of Dramatic Art (NIDA) Short Course Program in Sydney offers members of the public classes in a wide variety of performance related activities from acting, to script writing, to design, to short film making and beyond. A new course recently introduced is the chance to be in a production. The budget for the production comes from course fees; therefore to make the production viable, the cast size needs to be around sixteen performers, all with roles of equitable size.

Jennifer Hagan, who agreed to be the play's director, has had a long association with NIDA both as a director and as a teacher. She also has a record as a well-known theatre performer and as a professional director of new work. We met in February 2008 and discussed structural changes to the draft to make the script more active, more visually engaging. Jenny also wanted new content that would create more ensemble opportunities for the cast. Together we pitched the project to NIDA in August 2008 and they agreed to offer it a production in February 2009 as part of their Short Course Program.

Once a production was guaranteed, I sourced more ensemble material. I went back to Lisa and asked her to describe the crash victim's funeral she had attended and I interviewed a trauma counsellor, who explained the healing process from a professional point of view. Prior to rehearsals I began a massive content restructure, aware that the expectations of a performance in a conventional theatre space are radically different from those of a performed reading. I had to get the actors on their feet; I had to create opportunities for them to engage with each other, as well as the audience; I had to double the cast size; and I had to keep the text verbatim.

The development of a rehearsal draft: *Remembering a Day in December*

To incorporate the new cast and the new material I embarked on a much more rigorous process of intercutting dialogue. I had been tentative doing this in *Remembering Glenbrook,* as I felt it allowed me to be unduly manipulative as a playwright. However, facing the demands of theatrical production and a large ensemble cast meant making new decisions. After four public readings I was also more confident that the play's content would be supported by character interaction. The rehearsal process also made it clear when characters' ideas or realisations were repeated and how this repetition was not advancing the dramatic narrative and therefore how the dramatic tension stagnated as a result.

The only major structural change at this point was a swap of Chapters one and two, so the play started with the shock of the collision. I also attempted to create a continuous text by eliminating the dependence on the chapter headings. I had become so familiar with the material, I was able to locate appropriate lines and where I couldn't, I went back to the original transcripts.

The content was now spread across more characters and there was new information. In *Remembering Glenbrook* Lisa mentions that Stu went to an art class, where:

> Lisa : *...they'd draw and they'd talk about feeling and things like that. Now even though that wasn't a highly professional group, it did seem to do something for him... after that he got this little bit of momentum to go back out into the workforce.*

Jenny, the director, thought that reconstructing the art class would help activate *Aftermath,* as the cast would be engaging with their inner creative life and their outer functional life with each other. The idea resonated strongly with the earlier demand for a de-brief. Although I couldn't construct an art class from the trauma counsellor's professional narrative, I was able to create multiple healing scenarios. By intercutting the participants' original narratives about counselling and introducing three different psychologist characters, I juxtaposed the characters' experiences with trauma theory. Because of the Justice archetype used earlier, the Psychologists' presence wasn't stylistically jarring.

Dave: So I eventually just went and saw the psychologist in Penrith, just paid for it, and I found just the simple thing of just getting that off my chest – I'd never really sat down and spoke to anyone about it, I probably didn't really do that with my wife, I was probably adopting the macho image of big men don't cry and trying to battle through it. It's just telling someone how I felt about that and how it affected me. It all came in a big rush to this psychologist. It was like just a big weight lifting off my shoulders.

Psych 1: The Talking Cure. It validates and accepts what has happened.

Rita: I went to Jane, the counsellor. And she said:

Psych 1: Just talk about it, Rita

Rita: And I did.

Psych 1: When it happened, how did you feel?

Rita: Shocked.

Psych 1: Then what did you feel?

Rita: Anger.

Psych 1: Then what did you feel?

Rita: Sadness. And I sat there and wept. And I think that was good, she walked me through all the steps.

Psych 3: More importantly the Talking Cure demands that the person looks within themselves to their strengths – to find the different Mes.

The final section became a kind of group therapy session. The characters addressed each other not the audience. They supported each other with *ad libs* and when they weren't speaking paced with a restless energy. The actors' physicality demonstrated inner turmoil, while their words grappled with their shifting perspectives. The play was on its feet.

Not only did the new content have to be shared, it also needed to be edited. By the time *Remembering a Day in December* was in its third week of a four week rehearsal period it was running at 75 minutes. Being present in rehearsal with the actors and the director strongly supported the editing process. As a researcher, I connected so strongly with the original participants that I felt like a privileged custodian of their stories. But as a playwright and performer, my relationship had to evolve. The play now had another community to serve, a community that now included students and industry professionals. The characters were composites; they spoke the original data with new meanings and a succinct economy. Some narratives were lost or diluted but key research revelations remained and the work became more precise.

In the final week of rehearsal the play, now running at 63 minutes after more refining, became *A Day in December*. In production, technical elements were introduced to support the director and designer's realisation of the script. Sound effects created the collision and were repeated at different times to reinforce the collision's recurring resonance for the characters; lighting effects emphasised the characters' isolation. Luggage strewn across the stage after the collision represented the emotional baggage of the passengers, which they slowly tried to incorporate back into their lives during the last section of the play. Another short film sequence bookended the play: trains pull into Glenbrook station, they rattle round the bends along the accident site, the film segments of the train are tranquil, it's an ordinary day. The repetition of this filmed sequence made a significant contribution to the production: seen at the beginning it localises the play, it helps set the scene; seen at the end its effect is haunting, it captures the arbitrary nature of disaster, one of the recurring themes that underpinned the participants' testimonies.

A Day in December had four performances in February 2009 and played to full houses. The cast was enthusiastic about the whole experience and loved the fact that their lines had been spoken by real people. The director and I agreed that I could make script changes up to two weeks before the first performance; after that it belonged to the cast and the production. I knew I had to step back and trust the material. Drama is a collaborative art form and my high regard for Jenny meant I had complete faith in the production process, Right from the beginning the participants' stories generated respect and empathy; these qualities were tangible in the rehearsal room and I hoped they would be there on stage.

A discovery

From its first public reading *Remembering Glenbrook* delivered un-expected and gratifying outcomes. Feedback revealed that the perfor-mance had created connections between what was said by the characters and what was felt by the audience. Consistent with observa-tions made by other researchers of performed data (Alexander, 2005; Mienczakowski, 2003) the play had therefore accentuated the larger cultural context in which the eight personal narratives were embedded.

The content appeared to have transformative elements, as all theatre should. The combination of the Public Inquiry and interwoven per-sonal narratives about despair and isolation, hope and resilience had created a new level of empathic awareness of the complexity of trauma, indicating, as Arnold (2005) suggests, that a higher learning had taken place. And by generating an empathic response, the performance had generated a journey inwards. Comments from all the casts that read the play and those that rehearsed and performed it, as well as comments from audience members, confirmed that insights particularly about trauma had been generated.

A Day in December has travelled a long way from the original research data but I see this journey as a continuum. I wanted to present my re-search as a verbatim theatre play. I wanted to investigate the verbatim theatre form from transcript to stage script. And I wanted to know the choices I would make as I attempted to meet the challenges of the form.

Verbatim theatre and the playwright's challenge

As verbatim text moves from research data towards theatrical produc-tion, questions about its authenticity become increasingly frequent. In my experience this is the time when the content comes under the greatest scrutiny and the original research runs the greatest risk of be-ing compromised. However, if one can accept that performance is already artificial, can one allow for degrees of authenticity?

There is an old adage appropriate here: we watch radio but we listen to television. When text is read, the reader is closely related to the story-teller, the original source of the data. Our imagination builds the pic-tures; as with radio, we 'see' the story individually. But television, film and theatre give us contexts, so for us to remain engaged, the demands on story content, non-verbal narrative elements and script structure increase. To remain compelling, the story has to be delivered with a momentum and intrigue far removed from the rhythms of recall and monologue. The way a story is told changes but does that dilute its veracity?

Fabrication is an integral component of performance. Characters in verbatim theatre represent participants; they might even be composites of different research contributors. Action that happened in the past has to navigate its way back to the present through imposed character relationships and action that happened over long periods of time has to occur within a fixed time frame. Though the text might be presenting multiple voices and multiple truths (Paget, 1987; Cheeseman, 2005), diversity is limited by theatrical constraints like time and dramatic structure. Finally, all decisions involve a playwright's bias.

I certainly found that over the entire arc of the verbatim theatre journey I became more flexible both in what was said when and who said it. Although I wanted all the text to originate from the transcripts, as the cast size grew and the need for inclusivity was paramount, I shifted lines between cast members, giving them the challenge of justifying them. Because the actors played multiple characters, I relied on their being identifiable within the play's action. I had guaranteed all my participants privacy, so I never intended that the characters would identify themselves, as practised in other verbatim plays like *The Laramie Project*. So, unintentionally I had given myself the freedom to be able to distribute the data without compromising any of my own chosen conventions.

Dialogue was only a problem for me, as a researcher, in *A Day in December*, when characters ad libbed to enhance dramatic conflict. This occurred particularly in the *Public Inquiry* and the final section of the play, the former *Aftermath*. But the energy generated by this kind of active participation completely supported the play; it reinforced the strength of the ensemble and by accentuating tension and suspense, increased the audience's receptivity. Over the four performances the verbal ad libbing became less articulate and the characters' physical restlessness increased. It was as if the actors' growing confidence allowed them to externalise their emotional responses to events in the play in a more dramatic way. I know that Jenny, the director, had encouraged this development in note sessions prior to each performance and I thought this evolving choreography was an inspired solution to the play's more difficult areas.

Watching the actors through the performed readings, in rehearsal and over several performances made me aware of how elusive characterisation and the performance style for verbatim theatre can be. Sensitive to caricature, interpretations need to be anchored in reality. However, the narrative can support a heightened level of performance intensity for the play's duration; certainly *A Day in December* was strengthened when those opportunities were taken.

In all performance scenarios the casts expressed a great respect for the dialogue, because 'it had been said by real people.' I sense that this encouraged identification with character, which enhanced the creative experience for actors of generating performance. They knew the play's world and shared it with their characters, with the ensemble and with their audiences.

Conclusion – learning from the experience

I believe verbatim theatre has a valuable contribution to make to performance ethnography and to the telling of community stories. For directors, writers and actors it gives a framework to research, create and perform stories that they might be aware of but may have considered too narrowly. Sharing new understandings with the community that generated the stories reinforces a sense of identity, enriches cultural awareness and supports new understandings of diversity. The form offers interesting possibilities particularly now, as web technology, multi-national media ownership and threats on a global scale have created common language, common concerns and broadened the concept of community itself.

My experience of *A Day in December* is that the verbatim form developed connections; the original research generated recognisable characters and their stories resonated empathically with audiences. Because it is concerned with multiple perspectives and multiple voices, the verbatim form also effortlessly embraced the demand for new content, as the play moved towards production. Distilled from a small group of commuters in the Blue Mountains, disparate informants in the field, the research outcome, the play, is concerned with the long, slow road to healing and demonstrates the universality of grief and loss.

My aim was to create a performed work that met the challenges to authenticity inherent in the verbatim theatre form, without sacrificing the work's integrity as a piece of theatre. In hindsight I feel I have achieved this with the generous support and invaluable expertise of colleagues. But I recognise that any performance is always a work in progress; it is always the product of multiple perspectives and inter-pretations. Nevertheless, I hope the project in its different manifes-tations makes a positive contribution to the diverse spectrum of perfor-mance ethnography.

9

SCRAP PICKERS AND OTHER LOCAL HONG KONG PROJECTS
Fast tracking ethnodrama: a two-week assignment in Hong Kong

Estella Wong, Phoebe Chan and their students:
Boey Chan, Natalie Cheung, Ralph Cheung, Winnie Chow,
Felix Du, Leung Ka Po, Ruby Kwan, Kenny Kwong, Louisa Lau,
Mabel Pi, Liu Pui Fong, Terrence Sin, Karley Ng, Krissy Lam,
Bettina So, Elayne Thong, Lena Lee, Karl Wickeremasuriya,
Lo Chi Yan; with detailed contributions from
Kate Allert and Will Liu

Introducing the case study

Since 2004, Griffith University and the Hong Kong Arts School have together delivered a Masters course in Drama Education in Hong Kong. The projects discussed in this case study were completed at an intensive summer school in 2005 as Performance Projects which are compulsory for year two students.

The course aimed to explore through ethnodrama the many natural connections and tensions between drama and theatre, education and research. Students first decided on their target research community, potential audience and, for this exercise, educational purpose. They then had to create a group-devised theatrical presentation, addressing the educational objective or purpose through careful selection of genre and style according to their purpose and their own performing abilities.

As in many ethnodrama projects, the participants were not all experienced actors or performers.

The five groups came up with different topics, research communities, target audience and educational purpose, identifying areas relevant and close to their experiences. Section 1 includes consideration of five ethnodramas with their creators' analyses. They review their processes in this time-restricted project, to what degree their own perspectives emerged in the finished pieces and whether they remained faithful to the data they gained during the research process. Their deliberations raise many of the issues central to this book. The thinking from all the groups is heard in Section 1. Section 2 focuses on a more detailed analysis of the process and outcomes of one of them, *The Scrap Pickers*, from two of its creators.

SECTION 1: The Projects

1   *The Scrap Pickers* sought to explore and present the predicament of elderly scrap pickers. Curious about the stories behind these silent and unnoticed outdoor workers, the team tried to understand their lives through interviews, social worker referrals and government documents. Their aims for the audience were specific. The performance was to constitute a Theatre in Education programme targeted for younger secondary students.

2   *Indonesian Domestic Maids* focused upon the maids working in Hong Kong who had been the subject of recent Hong Kong media coverage. The group tried to get a fuller picture of the issue from different perspectives by collecting data from the abused Indonesian maids themselves, the consul, the employment agent, relevant government organisations and the employers. Scenes of how misunderstanding or conflicts arose from cultural differences and different ways of carrying out domestic work were presented. Statistics and facts were also introduced inbetween scenes. The group identified potential employers of Indonesian maids as their target audience,. Their educational purpose was to increase the mutual understanding between the employer and the maid, to eradicate or reduce conflict and abuse.

3 *One Size* concerned people trying to lose weight. The group responded to a sense that slim culture has been sweeping through the world and Hong Kong is no exception. Although slim does not necessarily mean fit, people are driven by the mass media, their spouses, colleagues, relatives and friends, and the fashion manufacturers, to try and mould themselves into a standard size, regardless of their physical build. The team sought to raise awareness of slim culture by inviting local audiences to reflect on their attitudes and by encouraging critical thinking about the issue.

4 *Online Game Player* was developed by a group who agreed that playing online games is widely perceived as a time consuming, money wasting, addictive and unconstructive activity. They intended to show the more private side of three game players of different genders, ages and backgrounds through revealing their everyday lives for the audience to find out what online games might mean to the players. The team saw their purpose as countering prejudice against online game playing by showing the positive effects it has on players' lives.

5 *DINKs*, those with double income and no kids, were the final group's target community. Starting with several interviews with DINKs, the team became stuck on a number of issues around the task of producing an ethnodrama. The focus then shifted from presenting DINKs' point of view to meta-research of ethnodrama itself. The presentation started with researcher-performers presenting in-role as DINKs, then jumping out of role to address the difficulties they themselves faced, their changes of perception of the topic, and their researchers' reflections on the DINKs issue. They identified their target audience as future students of this ethnodrama project and sought to stimulate reflection on the factors which might affect the interpretation of research findings in an ethnodrama.

The context of choice

The students came to their decisions about which subject to research from a range of contexts and ideologies. Their comments highlight the way that researchers are initially tied into their own positions and how their individual contributions have been shaped by their lives, and how their research experiences have reshaped their thinking.

The letters after the contributor's name identify which ethnodrama they have been involved in:

S: *The Scrap Pickers*
M: *Indonesian Domestic Maids*
Z: *One Size*
O: *Online Game Players*
D: *DINKs*

Lena[D]:	For our group, I believe our different marital status is impacting on our perspective. Bettina is a single theatre worker; having kids is probably a remote issue for her. Jonathan is actually a DINK himself in his late 30s, and it's a critical moment for him to reconfirm his decision. Felix is a happy father and husband with a fifteen month-old son, and I am a working mother, married for twenty years, with a fourteen year-old son. Our different backgrounds affect our perspectives on DINKs as well as what we want to get from this research. Take myself as an example: I have to admit that at the outset my purpose was to 'change the perception of some DINKs' but after the whole process, I have gained respect towards DINKs and their choice.
Bettina[D]:	My background as professional theatre director and actor also affected my role in the project. I was active in giving artistic advice on the dramatic set up, plot and content, which aimed at a more effective theatrical expression of our ideas and data.
Kate[S] :	Our group members were very interested in welfare issues, whether animals or humans, but we soon started focusing more on human issues, since my own heavy involvement with animal welfare might have influenced the project. Besides, my British background and outsider viewpoint were relevant when we were developing the project. There are no elderly people in the UK working like this (not in the public eye, anyway) and so many aspects of this group of people struck me very strongly, which the others would not have found remarkable because they had grown up in Hong Kong society and had seen this all their lives. Also, I live on Lamma Island, where a number of elderly people make extra money from collecting scrap. I knew one woman very well, as she had been my neighbour for a couple of years. These women's situations are very different from their urban counterparts and they proved to be much more approachable, so we were able to talk with them at

length and gain some insights into their lives in a rural environment.

Louisa[M]: I think personal networks affected our choice of the project. One of my friends was a ministry worker with Indonesian maids; not only could she provide information and share her viewpoint on the issue with us, she could also line up potential maids for our interviews. Furthermore, one of our group, Karl, is an English speaker who doesn't understand Cantonese. Researching on Indonesian maids allowed him to take part without any language barrier at all.

Ka Po[M]: Karl could speak the Indonesian dialect which helped a lot in interviewing the maids who do not speak English. For me, never having had an Indonesian maid I could be quite neutral and objective about the conflict between the maids and their employers.

Mabel[M]: As we Chinese emphasise the importance of the family unit, I have always wondered how the maids manage to leave their families for years to work in Hong Kong for $HK3000-4000 a month.

Chi Yan[Z]: For our group, most of us preferred a less serious topic. So when the idea of researching slim culture came up, everyone was happy and agreed on it immediately.

Having explained the influence of their personal experiences and attitudes in the project, the researchers then considered how their own positions were presented in the performances and how they conceptualised their roles as researchers.

Mabel[M]: I guess my position was presented in the storyline of the maids leaving their families to work here where lots of miscommunication took place.

Elayne[M]: As we wanted to give Hong Kong employers a better understanding of their newly acquired helpers, we decided to show them a typical Indonesian village home where the maid spoke Malay, ate with her hands and had never worked with electrical equipment such as vacuum cleaners and rice cookers. So we came up with the roles of an Indonesian maid, her husband and her employers, a typical Hong Kong couple. We also brought in neutral voices of NGO, social worker and maids' agent .

Louisa[M]: We tried to present the issue as objectively as possible by trying to show that everyone had their own reasons for their thoughts and behaviour; we didn't assign responsibility for the problem. We tried to show potential employers that they should be well prepared before deciding to employ the Indonesian maids.

Ruby[S]: As researcher, I felt comfortable during the acting, confident in honouring our data since we had put all our effort into preparing the project.

Kate[S]: I played one character to type, as an expat ranting about how unforgivable it was that a rich society like Hong Kong allowed the workers, who had helped make the city great, to live in such hardship. It didn't totally represent my position – my feeling that the social isolation and hidden poverty that many elderly people experience in Britain is just as bad as Hong Kong. I would have liked, with a longer piece with more time, to pose the question to the students: which did they think was worse? Utter loneliness, but with your basic needs covered, or needing to labour hard in your old age, but with plenty of interaction as a side-effect?

Kenny[Z]: Regarding our project, *One Size*, I am critical of what I call the beauty standard set by the companies in the keep fit business. They advertise that the beauty standard is having a slim body, so people who want to achieve it will try their best to become slim through an excessive amount of exercise. I created scenes by illustrating the data collected: for example, that the primary reason for exercising was to become slim in order to be accepted by people around them.

Winnie[Z]: As researchers, the data told us that people are pursuing slimness for a pretty appearance and appreciation from people around them, while fatness always brings embarrassment. As directors and educators, we want to increase awareness of our own involvement in creating the slim culture consciously and sub-consciously in our everyday lives. We created a detective investigating what caused our victim's death by collecting data and evidence; we figured the detective role is much the same as the researcher. In the performance, the detective used photos, tape recorder, materials such as a dancer's costume, a peeler, a piece of carrot etc., to stimulate audience's thoughts and reflections.

Kate acknowledges her UK perspective, while Ruby feels comforted in her knowledge that the group were honouring the data they presented in their ethnodrama. It is clear that there are different perspectives on all the topics, so the students consider how they represented different (researcher) interpretations of the data, and tried to convey them authentically. When considering how they could represent the data, they were advised to think about how truth is defined. They all wanted to present the data in a way that did not change it from how they had received it, yet that sometimes clashed with the need to ensure that the subject was presented in a balanced way. The students knew they were expected to avoid value judgements but found it difficult to do so. Their voices express their struggle to find the most appropriate and fair way to interpret their research data and attempt to apply it to their performance project.

Ka Po[M]: Our data came from a variety of sources, including new maids, consul, agent, different government organisations, employers and abused maids. We came clean and tried not to be biased. We anticipated that people generally were very sympathetic to the abused maids and perhaps critical of the employers. But we wanted to be fair to both parties. We did find other sides to the story that the general public might not know: for instance, agents lose money as compensation for irresponsible maids; and the majority of maids are satisfied with their present situations, even though people generally thought that they were suffering. We verified and cross-checked our data from all accessible sources. Interpreting it, we took into account the motivations and standpoints of all the interviewees.

Elayne[M]: We did not represent different interpretations of the data. We just walked the tightrope striving to ensure our data was objective and unbiased, accurate and clear: that the maid was not seen as too pitiful or the employer too abusive. We hoped the audience would realise that neither party was necessarily at fault, but each needed to understand and work with or round the other's differences.

Elayne[M]: Since all of us started out sympathetic towards maids, especially when we saw the photos of abused maids, we kept reminding each other that we had to be objective. Having team mates look out for each other helped a lot. We also tried to validate our data by scrutinising every piece of data carefully and cross-checking it constantly. For example, after we conducted our interviews with the maid agency chairman, we tallied his figures with information gleaned from research from newspapers articles and websites. Then we avoided words that were emotional, especially in quotations taken from our interviews with the abused maids and the social worker.

Ruby[S]: With quite a number of field observation notes, I thought of 'real case' presentation for authenticity. When we were polishing the data artistically, we kept reminding each other to consider questions such as 'Would the change in presentation convey the meaning we really want?' and 'What would an ordinary audience make of our performance choices?'

Kate[S]: Ralph and I played researchers who were terrified of approaching their subjects! This was true. We were all very concerned about appearing to be patronising, or that we were nosing into their hardship without offering solutions. We tried very hard to just present the data honestly, as we had received it from the subjects, in order to leave it as open as possible for student interpretation.

Ruby [S] : I prefer to present words from paper neutrally, then add in our opinions too. It is important for the audience to distinguish between the data and our comments.

Kate[S]: It would be naïve to think that the final piece contained no value judgement from us: the choice of our data and the structure of the piece must reveal something about our standpoints. However, everything included was thoroughly discussed and agreed by us all, so I do think we kept ourselves out of it as much as we could. The Theatre in Education format was specifically chosen for the students to develop their own opinions, not be presented with ours.

Kenny[Z] : I held three interviews with my interviewee to avoid value judgements. Sometimes, I tended to interpret the meaning of data through my own experience or beliefs. For example, I hate those companies promoting so-called keep fit concepts and getting the most benefit from doing this. Aware that my value judgement could easily lead me to misinterpretation, I would always remind myself to keep neutral by asking clarifying questions, and re-phrasing them before asking them in the next interview.

Winnie [Z] :   Although we can try our best to avoid value judgement, it is not possible to be one hundred per cent clear. What we can do is to leave more space for the audience to feel, think and judge for themselves. As educators with educational purposes in mind, what we present is already showing our value judgement: for example we want a society accepting of diversity. I think the dramatic metaphor can also help us to avoid value judgement. The audience need to think and re-think the message presented and the post-performance discussion and exhibition can also help them to discuss and further explore the issue.

Terrence[O]:   I tried to avoid value judgements in the early stage in the interviews and the case study itself. I tried to contribute to 'dancing the data', by attempting just to focus objectively on what I got from the case. That's why I chose to use a realistic style for the performance. For me an abstract style would imply value judgements in interpretation.

Chi Yan[Z]:   Our group tried not to ask directive questions in the interviews and when we reported back the data to the group, we tried hard to preserve the interviewees' original attitudes.

Natalie[Z]:   We paid progressively more attention to the messages presented by artistic choices such as different movement or facial expression. For example, in the mass media scene highlight where Pui Fong was dancing with her belly showing and captured by a camera, we discussed extensively whether the dancer should smile, look sad or be neutral, as well as her gesture, movement, pace and tone of voice. I thought the decision was important. Although we didn't intend to make judgements or take sides on the keep fit business, each facial expression would suggest a different interpretation for the audience and would also reflect our viewpoint. The dancer smiling might lead the audience to think she enjoyed her belly being captured.

Bettina [D] :   I avoided value judgements by staying aware of the distinction between data analysis and personal perceptions. To avoid choosing topics with conflict of interest amongst group members would also help.

These ethnodramatists were working to an assignment task and knew the criteria for assessment. This could have put specific pressures on their work. However, they suggest that it was the two week time limit, much tighter than usual for this kind of work, that imposed most pressure.

Ruby [S]: We were so busy collecting data and devising, we just totally neglected the terms of the assignment! I think the pressure did not come from the grading, but from the time constraint.

Elayne[M]: I don't think that its being part of our assessment affected us. With only a few weeks to complete the project from the beginning of the research till the actual performance, even less as most of the team members were working full-time, we could only skim the surface of the issue. While doing our research we did come across other very interesting issues, which we had no time to explore. Lack of time also affected the number of interviewees. As the performance date approached, we also had to trim down our ethnodrama and ended up opting for a simple, stylised play, juxtaposing two scenes. We had to give ourselves artistic license to imagine what an Indonesian maid's husband was like back in her village: with no time to research it, we relied on symbols such as rice, or rather lack of it, to show poverty and a sarong to represent those things that we guessed would be important to her.

Bettina[D]: On the positive side, having an assignment gave us a clear direction. It also enhanced our group spirit and team work by requiring every team member to give our best. We created it through truthful discussion and compromises with mutual trust.

Chi Yan[Z]: Since it was an assignment, we took everything seriously, such as data collecting, how to honour the data and reflecting on the whole process.

Winnie[Z]: We all wanted to make our performance more artistic, partly due to the marking scheme of this performance project and partly because we believe in the power of theatre.

Section 2 : The Scrap Pickers project

Kate: The main community we studied was that group of elderly Hong Kong people who scrape a living by collecting various forms of scrap and receive small amounts of money for doing so. We also studied ourselves as very inexperienced and rather scared researchers. Finally we included a witness character who amalgamated our own viewpoints as liberal thinkers questioning how such a situation could exist in this day and age.

This section provides a close focus on the Scrap Pickers project. Part A looks at the student ethnodramatists themselves, their motives and intentions. Part B explains the project as it was delivered for secondary school pupils, including a synopsis of the performance. In Part C two of the students, Kate and Will, give their analyses of the project.

A) Aims – personal and social

The four members of this group were all involved in the project as researchers, devisers and performers. Coincidently, two are specialists in education and two in theatre. Their backgrounds are diverse. Ralph is a graduate of Hong Kong Academy for Performing Arts, currently teaching extra-curricular drama classes in youth centres and schools. Kate is an English teacher and drama graduate with experience of working on drama projects with high security life prisoners in the UK. Ruby is a secondary Physical Education teacher who also leads an extra-curricular drama club. Will is a secondary English and Liberal Studies teacher and also a member of the counselling team.

Will: To us, the scrap pickers are our research subjects, not participants, because most of them don't understand what we are trying to do. I believe they just thought we were casually chatting when we interviewed them. A few of them got a bit scared when we revealed we were collecting information. I doubt that many, if any, would care to see or participate in the performance. This was the main tension in the project. If we explained too much, these old people would get more doubts and worries and become too shy to talk. But when we talked as a casual chat, many were more willing to share their stories. So our technique was to mention our intention briefly to them and then quickly move into the chat. We should have first built relationships with them, but it was impossible in the research time frame. I felt that it was a bit like stealing information but we tried our best to be fair, and report and perform their responses as realistically as possible.

Kate: All of us agreed from the beginning that we wanted to work on something with social relevance. We all had experience in using drama either with or for groups in society with particular needs. Our first few choices of topic had to be discounted, constrained by the fact that we were student researchers. Some of the groups we were interested in researching were too vulnerable to let us approach them or for their social workers to take our request seriously.

Will: Teaching English and Liberal Studies, my main motivation was to create an activity/performance that helped students who were our target audience to explore the world: to paraphrase our lecturers, to bring the life of one community to another. In our case, it was to bring the life of scrap pickers to secondary students for them to develop an understanding and hopefully to care about other communities in our society. We also soon found that the project could be a vehicle to promote moral and value development.

Ruby: The project was an assignment of the Masters course which I *had* to finish. Yet, the nature of its theatrical presentation aroused my interest and motivated me to contribute my best. It also enhanced my own development in drama education, using different dramatic forms and conventions. The free choice of topic also provided us with autonomy and creative space which I enjoyed very much.

Kate: I think Ralph and I, brand new to the course, were led totally by our professional drama experience. We wanted to create a piece of drama that worked in its own right and we wanted to honour our data in the way that it was presented to us by our tutor, Phoebe.

B) The project plan

The project was designed as part of a Theatre in Education programme targeting 13-14 year-old secondary students. It posed the question, 'Is the scrap picking business a way that improves the elderly's income, or are we exploiting them?' as a critical thinking and reflection topic. The programme began with a pre-task for the pupils, then the performance was followed by a post-show activity.

Pre-performance

The pre-task encourages the students to reconsider their attitudes to the working elderly in Hong Kong and the issue of recycling. They are allocated roles and asked to do some preliminary research from recommended sources. The students' roles include: Environment Activists,

Senior Government Officers, Social Workers working for the elderly and Waste Paper itself.

Prologue

The performance opens with still shots of elderly scrap pickers. Then two nervous researchers appear looking for some target interviewees. Finally they see an old man and an old woman, hard at work, pluck up courage to approach them but are rejected and disappointedly leave the stage.

Scene 1

Old Wong and Old Leung are playing Chinese chess. Leung cannot concentrate. He has had another row with his son-in-law and threatens to move out of the family home. Wong asks him how he can survive. Leung says he could manage on the monthly $700 'fruit money' that the government gives everyone over 65, plus what he could make by collecting cardboard boxes on the street. Wong points out that he would make only 40 cents a kilo these days, compared to $1 a kilo before the recession. Leung says some things are more important than money and points out that Ms Q, who has just turned up to sell second-hand goods on the street, looks proud, free and vigorous and he could be like her. Old Wong continues to give Leung a hard time, telling him that the paper shop exploits old people and the work is hard and dirty. People must stay flexible says Leung, just like his friend Chan who lost his job two years ago, but will not take government security money so will do anything to earn a few dollars. Wong bemoans the situation, saying that Hong Kong citizens deserve a better deal, then heads off for lunch with his unmarried daughter.

Scene 2

A western woman, reading her paper during this scene, notices Ms Q and expresses disgust that old people have to work so hard in a wealthy society like Hong Kong. She wonders what the government is doing.

Scene 3

Old Leung goes over to look at Ms Q's second-hand goods and they chat. He finds that Ms Q, who is 86 now, was an office cleaner till 1997, and discovers that she feels better working on the street than staying at home alone because she can talk to people and many people bring her things to sell. However, she complains that she sometimes has to make ten trips in the evening to take all her stuff up to her flat. When he asks her why she does not take government social security money she warns that this money brings bad luck as her cousin died the year after he started taking money from the government. Then Old Leung is surprised to find that she is supported by her son so and she is working to earn money to support her other grandchildren in China. He thinks maybe he could work like her. Then Ms Q sees a policeman and hurries away with her bags, complaining that the police give her trouble several times a day, driving her away from under the fly-over.

Scene 4

Enter two government figures: Longhair, local ex-activist, gives his usual rant about equality for all, while the Chair of the Legislative Council Environment Committee explains her solution to the recycling problem: allowing the elderly pickers to empty the government recycling bins and sell the contents, thus giving them an income and saving the government money.

Scene 5

The Cardboard Box, which has been centre stage throughout, comments on its own life, while Mr. Ancient slowly picks it up, folds it flat, then pours water in the middle of it so it will weigh more at the recycling shop.

Scene 6

Enter old Ms Ho and a researcher. Ms Ho is happy to talk. Her life is good. Although where she lives is pretty awful and she tries to stay out as long as possible, social workers are looking after her and trying to find her a new place. Besides, all her meals at an elderly centre cost only $HK20 per day. She comes down here to help her best friend, Mrs Ancient, who is paid by a government subcontractor to sweep the streets around here. The Ancients also collect cardboard boxes to sell as they are really very poor. Ms Ho encourages the researcher to approach Mrs Ancient but when he does, he is firmly rejected.

Scene 7

Shots of Lamma Island and the house of Ah Heung, who collects scrap metal and sells it to mainlanders who occasionally come in on a boat. The researcher tells us how she came to know Ah Heung and they chat. Ah Heung is 76 but still very active. She receives a small government pension since she was a cleaner but chooses to collect scrap metal from all over the island to make a little extra money for *yum cha* (traditional Chinese brunch). It is hard physical work and her knees get sore. It annoys her that the police and the marine police try to stop the boat coming in to buy her stuff. She is doing the government a favour by cleaning up metal which would otherwise end up as landfill so she wonders why they try to stop her. She makes only $10 for a trolley full of window frames. Her sons were not successful at school and are now construction workers who cannot help her out. Her greatest wish for the future is that her grandchildren are wise and good people.

Epilogue

Re-enter the two researchers. They address the audience directly. They deliver some hard facts about the situation in Hong Kong regarding the elderly and their role in the recycling industry and pose some questions. The final fact is that by 2033, one person in four in Hong Kong will be over 65 years old.

Post-performance

The students share what they have learnt from their preliminary research and discuss this in relation to what they have learned from the show. Then, in groups, they research further and debate the issues raised. They reunite to present their summaries of the individual debates possibly at least partly in dramatic form and finally write reflections.

The group now wishes to take their work beyond the university classroom, feeling strongly about the subject of their project. They would like to see the work performed for students studying social education, and to Hong Kong politicians involved in social welfare and environmental issues.

C) Participants' critical reflections

[Editors' note: Kate's and Will's original drafts contained much thoughtful, scholarly debate, clearly demonstrating how the contributors' practice was both enriched by, and sometimes challenged, the literature. Word limits have reluctantly forced us to omit most of this, since both the literature and their own insights have informed our framing chapters and their observations here offer further illumination.]

Kate

An analysis of the strengths and weaknesses of *The Scrap Pickers* serves to clarify the journeys between aims and intentions, artistic endeavour and the contexts of such projects. I have found that the degree of success achieved by *The Scrap Pickers* varies according to whose definition I apply.

I am particularly interested in the roots of ethnodrama as a tool for budding anthropologists so that they can gain the kinaesthetic experience of existence in another culture that broadens their understanding in a way that traditional study cannot. It allows them, as far as possible, to break out of the frame of reference they have inherited from their own culture. When I studied in drama school we had a taste of this when a particularly enlightened tutor had us spend every Saturday morning for an entire term in a twilit basement room. We had to create our own tribe, complete with customs, rituals and day-to-day practices, which we would inform by research into indigenous cultures during the intervening weekdays. While this culminated in me, as high priestess, sacrificing my future brother-in-law with a plastic spoon, the recollection of which never fails to bring a smile to my face, this exercise grounded our acting practice kinaesthetically in a unique way. We were left with another framework through which to recreate the reality of character and culture.

This leads to one of my biggest issues, perhaps irresolvable, with ethnodrama for the purpose of performance to a chosen audience; the experience of watching an ethnographic performance can never replicate that of taking part in it. For the researcher/performers, creating such a performance is an outstanding way to analyse and internalise research findings. I can see that there might also be immense benefit to be gained from presenting the resulting performance to the research participants themselves, to create a unique dialectic between them and their researchers. However, an ethnodrama which is created to be performed for a third party will always be fraught. Not only will that third party audience have their experience of the drama limited to watching it but also the reality they are observing is fatally compromised. The ethnodrama is the final product of various levels of interpretation: by participants of their own lives and of what they believe their researchers want to know about them; by the researchers and by the performers. In

The Scrap Pickers, we as researcher/performers learned a huge amount about our participants from observation, research and interview. Staging this knowledge gave us that additional, unique kinaesthetic experience.

A comment made in the post-performance discussion of *The Scrap Pickers* was that it came across as a documentary. I believe this comment justifiably raises the question: was *The Scrap Pickers* truly an ethnodrama or a piece of documentary theatre? In one sense *The Scrap Pickers* is firmly within the canon of documentary style performances. We presented research data verbatim, located firmly in the past when that data was gathered. We gave nothing back to our informants, nor did we recognise in the performance the audience's involvement at the moment of presentation. On the other hand, *The Scrap Pickers* did attempt to show the daily, ongoing reality of its participants and even give the audience the opportunity to experience some 'liminal moments' in terms of their own experience, and even perhaps 'epiphany', to use terms from the literature.

Our choice of the elderly, impoverished scrap pickers as subjects made it difficult to give the informants any opportunity to co-construct or control the text or the representation of themselves. This group's generally low education level and self-esteem, that we perceived and a social worker verified, made any involvement by them problematic. The few who were willing even to talk to us knew only that we were research students, as we believed that going into detail about our intentions for their data might confuse them and cause them to withdraw. Once interviews were completed, there was no further contact with them, denying them the opportunity to control text or representation. Even if we had chosen a more articulate and confident subject group, our own inexperience would have made us fearful of allowing them that kind of involvement. We felt barely in control of presenting the data ourselves; to have allowed any element of informant control was beyond our capabilities at that time.

This was exacerbated by our task itself: an academic exercise with no purpose beyond the educational for the researcher/performers. This put us at a grave disadvantage in terms of approaching our informants and the social workers who were expert in the issues of the scrap pickers, who were a disadvantaged group. You would expect research to be conducted to educate those who could alleviate their plight. We were aware how easily we could be perceived by both informants and social workers as dilettantes in an area of grave social concern. This, more than any indication, inhibited us from extending the scope of our research and their involvement. *The Scrap Pickers* suffered from not having access to 'validatory processes' from project participants and could undoubtedly have benefited from Bakhtinian dialogic interaction, to ensure that the voices of our participants were being as authentically represented as possible (Bakhtin, 1981). However, in spite of our limitations, we did try to expose oppression and challenge the existing social order through an artistic rendering of moral and political discourse. However, our target audience was not identified before the research commenced. We researched for a time, then matched our findings with the target audience we perceived to be the best fit.

We didn't make full use of the range of theatrical tools available to us. We chose very literal modes of expression and movement, with the exception of the stylised researchers in the opening sequence. We felt the issue itself was heavy enough for our target audience, presumably unexposed to much previous theatre. In retrospect our lack of experience and confidence in those modes of theatrical expression also inhibited us. Reading of much more physically symbolic, even choreographed ethnodramas I felt strong regret that we didn't do more with the physicality of the piece, such as observing and trying to recreate the specific physical reality of an elderly person doing this work. Verbally I regret our choice to be so literal throughout, rather than symbolic, even lyrical. While I still believe that it was important for the interviews to be verbatim, we could have been more creative with the other dialogue. That said, our 'two old geezers' scene was a theatrically creative solution to convey certain information. I think we could have pushed the humour and irony further, especially to make it accessible and interesting for our target audience. Earlier incarnations of the geezers scene were much funnier and more ironic, which was our natural instinct but fear arising from lack of experience in the field and a desire to get it right for the assignment led us to pull it back.

We have already noted the limitations imposed by time. Ethnographic performances presented by experts in the field are developed over months. *The Scrap Pickers* was conceived of, researched, devised and presented within a matter of days. Those responsible for it were learning on the job, so I am comfortable to conclude that as a piece of work with ambitions to be an ethnodrama it failed in several key areas but succeeded in others and fulfilled the demands of the academic exercise.

What then of the areas in which *The Scrap Pickers* succeeded? Audience members declared themselves moved by our presentation, with a new awareness of the plight of these people, which contributed to our participants' voices being heard, which is one of the established purposes of ethnodramatic representation. We worked hard to create evocative text, both in terms of editing participant interviews and creating original script, being mindful that our brief was also to be aware of our own biases and prejudices. A good example of our efforts to balance the two was in our presentation of information gained from Legislative Council Environment Committee minutes. We translated the comment by the Chair directly from Cantonese to English and presented it almost verbatim, with the addition of the words 'I've had a really good idea!' This was to alert audience members that this represented one woman's opinion only, not a standpoint endorsed by the Committee as a whole. How we chose to play this woman revealed elements of her personal style and left interpretation open as to the validity of her opinion. People reacted divergently to her statement that allowing the elderly impoverished to gather recyclables from the government recycling bins (currently illegal) would not only give them a small income but also save the government money. Some were horrified at her naivety, while others applauded her honesty. Either way, that segment was definitely evocative and provocative.

Creating on-stage verisimilitude was something that we took very seriously. Our research had given us a strong kinaesthetic sense of the physical reality of our informant group experience and our experience as performing artists gave us the techniques to reproduce that reality. The montage of real pickers in their environments set the scene before the actors emerged; the careful blocking and reproduction of movement and physical restrictions, along with appropriate costumes and props, helped achieve this. In an ideal world, I would have liked to include the constant background noise of heavy traffic and voices shouting to be heard over it. If physically possible, the smell of rotting vegetables, wet cardboard and traffic fumes would have enhanced the audience's experience even further, though probably not their enjoyment. I still feel unsure about epiphanies, since an epiphany seems to be a contradiction of daily reality. I can only hope that the questions we asked and the information we presented portrayed the essence of our participants' experience, while staying true to the minutiae of their daily lives, creating an epiphany for the audience, though not for the informants.

Although I felt that *The Scrap Pickers* could have been more theatrically adventurous, the piece had a theatrical unity, thanks to the backgrounds of Ralph and myself as performing artists before we became researcher/educators. This was facilitated by Ruby and Will's willingness to 'play' with us, which must have been influenced by their experience with process drama during the first year of their Masters' study. We had a performative edge, and this was commented on in the after-show discussion.

Will

I want to examine the tensions and relationships between the three dimensions of research, art form and education and evaluate how my group handled them in our ethnodrama project. First, I look at the relationship between education and research and then in more depth about these in relation to drama, the art form.

The relationship between education and research

Our project was an example of an ethnodrama where the educational purposes directed the research and the enquiry process, and data collected enriched and modified the educational potential. We were surprised to realise our project's great potential only after we had started our research, with our intention to discover and disseminate new information about an important social issue. I was inspired by Dan Baron Cohen's keynote address at the Planting Ideas in Asian Cities Drama Conference 2005, to use our project to help build understanding and care between different communities in our society. We soon settled on the study of elderly scrap pickers on the street. The initial literature review reinforced our determination:, we found very few studies on these street pickers and there are no government departments or charity groups overseeing their needs.

Then some surprising findings pushed us to make further use of our data to generate a critical question for our intended audience of junior secondary students: 'Is the scrap picking business a way that improves the elderly's income or are we exploiting them?' Our education purpose would extend beyond improving understanding and care, to thinking critically about this social issue.

Not only did we learn about ethnographic research, we also found ourselves becoming more fascinated by and engaged with our project as we went on gathering, analysing and dramatising the data. The findings were far beyond our expectations and our perception of our case study informants was shaken and then changed. In other words, before our project went out to educate our intended audience, we found ourselves educated first.

The relationship between drama and research

Research data provides the content for the drama while the drama aims to re-present the data in a way that maintains not only the dimensions of the original interaction but more importantly the essence and spirit of the data.

The research data provided answers to some or all of the five Ws of drama: When, Where, What, Who and What's at stake. Then the structure, in other words the plot and storyline of the drama, were constructed. We analysed our data and selected what was most revealing and what related to our educational purposes. Then we tried to discover links between these pieces of data, sequence them and dramatise them. Saldaña's advice that 'An ethnodrama is the data corpus with all the boring parts taken out' (2003:221) is a demand of the art form which is sometimes difficult to fulfil because we should not and could not omit important but less interesting or digestible data. Luckily for us in this project, most important pieces of data carried surprises and dramatic impacts. All we had to do was sequence the data and invent some lighter scenes among the denser ones. Besides, as most of our pieces of selected data were interesting by themselves, we did not try to twist them and fit them into a narrative with a linear development. Instead we kept mini-episodes of events that echoed or contrasted with each other. We believed that such a structure, highlighting our own absorbing interactions with the participants, would stimulate the audience's interest and critical thinking in the same way. Consequently we kept two researchers as characters in the performance, who also helped us define the context.

Just as the research data enriches the art form, so drama can enrich the representation of the research data, by effectively reliving the multidimensional meanings of research data. I believe drama can present the visual, aural, cognitive and affective aspects of research data holistically, to facilitate deeper and better informed understanding of the people and issues under study. Contrary to some authorities, I believe that accuracy, not imaginative understanding, is the core concern of ethnodrama and in our project the need to represent the data accurately was a high priority. This may be because our own perception had been so significantly changed by the raw data we found, that we assumed our intended audience would feel the same impact that we had experienced during our research. The feedback from our classmates, who were the practice audience of our project, confirmed our hunch; many said they were moved and that they had been given a different perspective on the issue.

The relationship between drama and educational purpose

Can drama educate and entertain at the same time as it ethically, honestly and accurately reports research? From my project experience and my reading, I found the two dimensions put certain limitations on each other but, given good design and structure, they could support each other and bring about wonderful effects.

In principle, the educational purposes of an ethnodrama can actually help the performance find a focus or structure, where every scene builds the dramatic impact towards bringing about the desired educational purposes. The various dramatic elements hook the audience and subtly guide them to focus on the desired educational issues. Although there may be conflicts between the need to educate and the need to entertain, the common element that brings the two together is the intended audience. If we understand the needs of the audience, we can use our resources,in other words our research findings and suitable dramatic treatment, to excite and inform them.

However in practice we found that it was not so easy. In our project, our intended audience was junior secondary students. Our goals were to promote their understanding of society by presenting them with a group of people whose lives were far removed from theirs and to improve their critical thinking ability by posing a challenging dilemma. We recognised that the students would not necessarily be interested in our research topic or our educational goals. Although we had confidence in the attractiveness of our data, we knew we still had to hook our audience and keep their attention throughout the 20 minute performance. Also, they might not feel connected to our research participants and would not identify with them. Our solution was to use the two researcher characters to give a highly stylised and exaggerated performance in the prologue to establish the context and arouse the students' curiosity. The two young researcher characters' nervous behaviour in front of their targeted informants and their difficult situation were like students' own feelings about their school project work. Lively music and video footage were played from the start. In the middle of the performance, a comic narration by a cardboard box was another feature which attracted attention, and made our audience feel at home with our performance.

Looking back, I think we were only partially successful because some of our audience doubted whether it would be interesting enough for the junior students. I think we could have changed some characters so that students could more readily identify with them. But we would have had to change a lot of scenes because we did not have enough performers to take up all the roles. Also, we had decided to keep some of the scenes which had the strongest research impact. Because of time limitation in preparation of the whole project, we could not crack all the difficulties we met.

However we did fairly well in resolving most of the tensions between the three dimensions of research, drama and education in our project, and we have learnt a great deal from the experience.

10

PERFORMING HISTORIES – VOICES OF BLACK RURAL COMMUNITY

From oral history to ethnodrama: the journey of the spoken word

Victor Ukaegbu
Jumai Ewu

Introduction

In March 2004 the Northampton Black History Project (NBHP), now Northampton Black History Association (NBHA), invited us to develop a stage performance from the information, personal stories and images generated from the organisation's oral history project on the presence of Black peoples in Northamptonshire. The project engaged members of the community as observers, as advisers and as participant and shaping artists.

Who Can Tell?...! is the story of us all, the different peoples and races that have settled in Britain through conquests, slavery, colonisation, and different waves of immigration. It recounts the histories of Black people and, though it is set in Northampton, it is a story that has been re-told and misrepresented by historians, the press and politicians throughout history. All too often these accounts are generalised and ignore individual experiences. *Who Can Tell?...!* tells both versions; it captures the struggles, the hopes, personal sacrifices and disappointments, the shattered dreams and heartaches experienced by immigrants and victims of mindless bigotry and racism everywhere. Crucially it celebrates their individual and collective triumphs. The play offers individual and group experiences of blackness and otherness and although set in a historical context the message and artistic provenance of the play transcend historical specificity. It portrays different stories of Black people told in historical truths rather than as historical exactitudes.

> *Family and friends gather for Maizie's big day, her surprise 60th birthday. As the guests arrive from different places memories of different experiences come to life. Maizie's experiences are sometimes hilarious and comic, sometimes serious and tragic, but it is the trajectory through which many colourful characters from different generations and backgrounds re-live aspects of Black people's histories from the heady 1960s to the present.*
>
> *The party is not all smiles; painful truths are confronted, a walk down memory lane reveals the anguish and tensions of race relations, broken lives, shattered dreams and some of those triumphs and joys that shape individual lives. The play invites the audience to join Maizie's party to celebrate and to reflect upon those moments and experiences that together make up our various collective histories.* (Synopsis of *Who Can Tell?...!* 25 May 2006)

Stories and marginalised communities

Tales of migration, peoples, and places have always provided a rich source of material for storytellers. Whatever their origins, stories are powerful cultural tools, whether recounted as fables, folktales, facts or fiction. When historicised in cultural and aesthetic terms the histories of people and races assume a different kind of significance. This is more so when such histories and stories are those of a marginalised group for whom the questions of ownership, authenticity and representation are equally important. Collective histories and personal stories change according to who recounts them, why they are re-told and the contexts of the telling. History, like all narratives associated with what Eagleton (1991) describes as 'identity thinking', is subject to many interpretations.

Some historical incidents and events acquire mythological status and are subsumed in the formation of racial identities. Such events as slavery, migrations, immigration, and race relations have contributed to how history presents the images of Black people in Northampton-shire. History is not only implicated in politics: narrative is a contested site and whoever controls it shapes how a people's history is presented and perceived. Whether intended or not, it is impossible to perform an apolitical history of a people or racial group within a larger cultural framework. By their nature, performances of group histories either conform to or operate outside the normative, aesthetic, and functional values of the dominant cultural system. Do the artistic shifts from histories to performance sites and the need to use one as a framework for the other carry responsibilities for the narrative, for the owners of the history and for the performance-makers? If so, how significant are the responsibilities? If we, as controllers of the narrative, inevitably shape it in performance and cultural terms, how can we ensure the owners of the stories do not feel their stories have been colonised, truncated or misrepresented?

The NBHP started in 2003 as 'a community-led initiative which aimed to gather, record, and promote the histories and stories of Northamptonshire's Black communities and individuals over the past 500 years' (NBHP, 2004:1). Our involvement derived from scholarly, artistic and ideological interests. As immigrants we all have stories to tell. The origin and nature of the source materials and their recurrent themes revealed things that intrigued and challenged us. Some of these include questions about collaboration, ownership, authenticity and the journey of the spoken word from research to the stage. We were challenged by how to compress five hundred years of Black history in Northamptonshire into a two hour stage performance without the risk of being as reductionist as the official version of history the project aimed to contest.

However, art is by nature ideological (Easthope and McGowan, 1992), none more so than theatre for 'the power to signify is not impartial either in the theatre (*sic*) or the world' (Hobsbaum, 1970:67). For this reason the project had to take a clear ideological and aesthetic stance on how best to transform oral interviews into performance.

Our aims were four-fold:

- to contest the stereotypical misrepresentation of Black people in British history

- to offer alternative narratives about the histories of Black presence in Northamptonshire

- to counter negative images of Black people through an interrogation about their experiences and their place in multi-cultural Britain

- to contest the notion of history as finished, fixed and isolated from the present.

The objectives were to use performance: to link the past with the present; to give Black people the opportunity to tell their own stories using their own cultural performance modes of presentation and aesthetics; to shift the perspective from story and history of Black people to stories and histories of Black peoples. These objectives required the performance project to interrogate official, received, and personal histories. It also had to deal with questions of ownership and authenticity, and managing ethical and cultural issues about the public and private, individual and collective, dimensions of the oral interviews, including using Northampton to represent Northamptonshire. The project involved active community participation and the performance was designed to be aesthetically accessible to members of the community.

The context of the initial research data and the project leaders

Unlike many ethnographic performance projects, we were not involved in the gathering of the research data, given to us at the outset by the NBHP. Taking on the data in this way gave rise to some difficulties. We were not party to the non-verbal cues in the interviews, nor did we have information on how the interviewees were selected or how random the selection process was. This raised questions as to how representative the interviews were of the experiences of Black people in Northamptonshire.

Summaries of transcripts and audio tapes of a random twenty two of the original interviews revealed several common themes and factors that have shaped Black people's histories and experiences of immigration to the UK. They identify the danger of generalisations of Black people's histories and differing reasons for immigration. Racial discrimination remained a factor for interviewees despite legislation and acknowledgment in several quarters that the UK is a multicultural, multi-ethnic society. Some struggled to define themselves because of their dual Black and British heritages. There are concerns that education has failed Black peoples and is especially guilty of perpetuating negative stereotypes; it is averse to the positive representation of Black people as role models and undermines their sense of worth and academic achievements. Contemporary concerns centred on political and economic limitations for Black people.

The research heightened our awareness of ethnic, gender and age differences in Black communities. For example, people of African and Caribbean backgrounds view themselves and each other differently in relation to slavery and migration. This manifests itself in intra-cultural tensions and perceptions that are overlooked in history's presentation of a homogenised Black experience and in the stereotypical misrepresentations of each other by African and Caribbean peoples.

Our sense of these differences, the lack of a single Black ideology and cultural perspective was sharpened very early in the project. We had assumed that as Black immigrants, we would be assimilated into other Black Northamptonshire groups. But we were outsiders because we had come from the University. Furthermore, we were from the county town, Northampton, which implies more privilege than Wellingborough, the second town involved in the project. We are both Africans and many participants are from the Caribbean, some are Black British of African and Caribbean descent, while some are white Caucasian. Within the two large regional groupings are Nigerians, Ghanaians, Jamaicans, Grenadians, Trinidadians and other nationalities and sub-groupings with distinct cultural and aesthetic differences. The same inter- and intra-cultural differences that exist among the various Black communities, who are so often lumped together under a label of 'Black People' were replicated in the project. However, by drawing creatively on these cultural differences, the group created a hybrid performance that addressed itself to various sections and ages of Black people. Instead of adopting a sole omniscient viewpoint, this lent itself to a collaborative working method.

Authenticity and risks of reductionism

The experiences of the interviewees from the original research were further supported by information and ideas derived from workshops in school settings to ensure young voices, missing in the interviews, were heard. Furthermore, the personal stories of all those involved in creating the performance provided additional research data. Hence, *Who Can Tell?...!* is the result of combined research by the NBHA and the performance-making group. The original interviews provided data, the workshops in schools and the on-going rehearsals of the project group provided further data as the work developed. This was not a project based on complete and fixed data. More information and ideas were produced through the performance process. Together we considered questions about the research: What is history and what makes it authentic? Does personal ownership of stories guarantee their authenticity? Recorded history often hides behind the cloak of authenticity without revealing that it is told from a given perspective. Personal stories, like histories, can be political and ideological; everything about history and personal stories is contestable. Through such debate the project engaged in critical dialogue about its materials and encouraged the audience to continue this dialogue in their engagements with the performance.

Bringing together voices from different sources presents additional issues of authenticity. Do those who are participant voices shape the voices of those before? What is authentic for whom? Authenticity is relative, difficult to define and means different things in different contexts. In a general sense it is the reliable and trustworthy recollection and representation of a group, person, object, idea, information, incident or event. In the context of this project it is social and relational, especially when the materials are viewed 'in and through relationships with tellers, spectators, and performers' (Rowe, 2007:175). Three roles are implicated in the transformation of Black histories and people's stories to the stage. For us authenticity is all about people representing themselves in their own worldview through their own images and cultural signifiers, irrespective of whether such representations are based on real life, on existential truths, facts, fiction, history, myth or even reconstruction of all of these. The materials are ethnographic and derive from and are about a people; their transformation for the stage can only be in a framework in which meanings reflect the concerns of Black communities and the strategies of representation are in line with their worldview.

The research was always influenced by artistic and ideological concerns and the need for authenticity. The work was experimental and required some degree of flexibility in terms of the performance theories, working methods, and theatre styles we drew upon at various stages of the process, such as theatre anthropology (Turner, 1991), Brecht's theory of historicisation and the technique of the alienation effect (Brecht, 1964), ethnographic (Mienczakowski, 1994) and verbatim (Paget, 1987) theatres, storytelling and documentary theatre, biographical styles, and from Playback theatre (Rowe, 2007). Underlining this eclectic methodology were the general principles and practices of participatory community theatre. Victor Turner sums up our experiences in transforming oral histories into stage performance:

> The most incisively or plainly reported case histories contained in ethnographies still have to be further distilled and abbreviated for the purpose of performance. To do this tellingly and effectively, sound knowledge of the salient socio-cultural contexts must combine with presentational skills to produce an effective playscript, one which effectively portrays both individual psychology and social process articulated in terms of the models provided by a particular culture. (Turner, 1991:109)

We had to be careful not to package the performance as the history nor to transform the experiences of communities or people into a representative emblem, but as a theatrical rendition of aspects of Black histories and the experiences of the many voices of the many peoples that were represented. In this respect the project was like playback theatre that 'is not just about the telling and dramatisation of personal stories, it is also concerned with, and sometimes a challenge to, accepted views concerning the boundaries between the personal and the public' (Rowe, 2007:45). Holderness (1992) points out that the 'responsibility of a progressive drama' is to challenge 'by showing that the existing order is not natural' but politically constructed and fundamentally unjust (p14).

It is insufficient for any marginalised group to contest its position of marginality by simply reclaiming its history as told by others. Stone-

Mediatore (2003) implies that the aim of an exercise such as the drama project that used a wide range of ethnographic materials about Black people should not simply be:

> to confirm (their) oppression but to affirm historical 'actors' that encompass heterogeneous and strategically chosen allegiances, historical 'actions' that are performed by people with limited public power and 'historical events', the impetus and significance of which are inseparable from so-called private lives. In so doing they do not only recast basic narrative categories but also help to build a resistant politics that is anchored in the realities of people's everyday lives (p143-144).

Artistic choices and tensions

There were many people who contributed to the artistic process. Rehearsals and performance workshops were open to members of the community. There were public discussion forums in two county towns, Northampton and Wellingborough and showings of work in progress. Local artists of diverse backgrounds were invited to contribute their particular skills to create a performance that reflected Black experiences and artistic conventions. Workshops in secondary schools and complementary research were undertaken to provide contemporary experiences and young voices.

Perhaps the most crucial challenge for us in this project was reaching a shared artistic vision for the work; the diverse training, professional and cultural backgrounds within the creative team threatened to pull the project in several directions. Artistic tensions and differences in professional, training and cultural backgrounds impacted on performance form and influenced the working process for the university-based participants and the collaborating professional artists. Those from the university favoured combining creativity with reflection, contrary to the collaborating artists' preference for artistic instinct without necessarily interrogating issues arising from aesthetic choices. The varied backgrounds impacted on performance form and influenced the working process. On the one hand there was the desire for a performance that used strategies of devising and constant dialogue with the material and with wider Black communities, and on the other hand the belief in solo-authorship of script.

The latter's preference for an Aristotelian model contested total theatre's all-inclusive framework characterised by episodic representation and the incorporation of other forms of performance and media. Most important for us was finding new and dynamic ways of working, roles and relationships that would be effective in the context of this particular project. We envisaged methods combining ensemble writing and making and storytelling. Storytelling theatre was an obvious choice. However, with different artistic perspectives, the first working script veered in the direction of dialogue drama as opposed to narrative drama. This impacted on our process. In place of communal creation based on improvisation and devising, the make-up of the creative team that included among others a stage director and a writer dictated a different approach to text development. Text development discussions emphasised the centrality of narrators operating within the context of total theatre. However, the emerging texts emphasised linearity and dialogue-based drama. Ultimately, it took considerable discussion and negotiation to shift from a naturalistic presentation to a storytelling style.

Starting with clearly defined aims posed it own dilemmas. Should ethno-performers work with artists and performers who share their aims and vision of performance or with whoever and whatever is available? How do ethno-performers and collaborators arrive at a shared vision for their performance and working process? Do dilemmas generated by differences in professional backgrounds impact on creativity and compromise artistic integrity?

These tensions were managed and resolved through continuous dialogue with the material and between members of the creative team, revisiting the aims of the NBHA and the adoption of an inclusive performance framework that incorporated features of total theatre, dialogue drama and multi-media. Community participation was central to the process and this took various forms at different stages. We opted for a holistic approach that not only took into account the oral interviews but involved a movement back and forth between an ever increasing core group and the wider community. The example of script development which follows gives an indication of how work journeyed through practice in a way that endeavoured to satisfy different artistic interests. The example shows a move from naturalistic to almost choric mode.

We ensured that the artistic license we exercised with the materials did not impair their authenticity and outcome as Turner (1991) has rightly argued. It did not change the perspective of the stories; the approach kept them and the performance within what NBHA and the project group define as Black cultural universe. The subjective, personal, and biographical voices associated with verbatim theatre ultimately gave way to the objectification of those voices, yet it enabled them to be critically interrogated and scrutinised.

Using the medium of performance was always going to pose its own theoretical and ethical questions; the intention to give voice evokes aspects of Playback Theatre. Rowe (2007) challenges performers in Playback Theatre to consider the details of personal stories they can share with the public. The project team debated Rowe's suggestion constantly but were aware that 'the individual spectator and the audience answer this question and how they draw the line between the personal and the public will be mediated by a complex interplay of subjective, relational and environmental factors operating in and around any particular venue' (Rowe, 2007:45). These factors include race, age, gender, artistic and professional backgrounds and personal experience.

The performance was in parts biographical, epic, naturalistic, and occasionally expressionistic, all contained in a flexible episodic storytelling framework. It accommodated other expressive forms such as music, dance, poetry, re-enactment and multi-media. This resulted in an interdisciplinary, integrative style that utilised the creative skills of collaborating artists and of members of the community. The approach integrated intensive rehearsals with moments of reflection on work in progress. As a result, both our thinking and doing were subject to change. Reflection was critical to the creative and social process and included how the team worked as a group, as well as what this said about the team and the nature of the project.

Script development

The process of transforming oral interviews into a performance script by the core creative team began with workshops and discussions aimed at facilitating a shared understanding of both the material and the project. Working from audio recordings of interviews and their transcriptions posed challenges. The draft working scripts were subject to deconstruction and reconstruction by the creative team, by contributions from participants at open readings, workshops and rehearsals and by the performers during the rehearsal process. The script was inspired by the source materials but not limited to them. The aim was to maintain dialogue with the material and to integrate moments of creative action with moments of reflection. Three draft working scripts were produced before intensive rehearsals and even then the script continued to evolve. From the character-based drama about a particular immigrant experience that was produced in the first working draft the script evolved into a performance text characterised by multiple narrators and an array of narrative voices.

Storytelling was a logical choice for us for several reasons: it is a popular form with direct links to oral history; its characteristic reliance on the dynamism of performers and their ability to quickly transform character, time, space, and action echoed some of the themes contained in the source materials. The episodic form lends itself to highlighting a selection of hot spots in an otherwise long chronicle of events and experiences, without necessarily losing a sense of the whole. The central storyteller was a woman, supported by a variety of other narrators, all of whom contributed to the narration and enactments of aspects of their stories. The main storyteller Maizie and the two young people to whom the stories were told provided a through-line that linked together past, present and future of Black experiences and histories.

Excerpts from different drafts provide useful examples of the journey of the spoken word from oral interview to the stage:

> *Doctor Prince Akamma is a proud African man dressed in his traditional outfit, from head to toe. He is tall and erect, having this regal presence about him, as if the prince in his name is not a mere name that sets him apart from all the Toms, Andys and Nigels in the world but a title, bestowed upon him by reason of who his father is.*
>
> *He walks slowly and inquiringly, looking this way and that, as if expecting his subjects to bow down and worship at his feet.*
>
> *There is that look of disdain about him for the space within which he finds himself, tantamount to scorn, his face contorted, as though something offensive is restricting his every breath.*

He scans the ceiling, the floor, wipes his finger along the wall and holds it up before his eyes, checking for dirt. He emits a sound, something between a groan, a growl and a sigh. His voice is a deep, rich baritone and, when he eventually speaks, his words carefully chosen to have their desired effects.

Doctor: This place is a tip. It is like a latrine.

 (He checks one chair after another for suitability before finally finding one worthy of seating himself on, still looking around).

Maizie: *(enters the room bearing tray with two glasses of drinks and a plate of sandwiches)*

 Sorry if I've been a little long. If I knew you were coming I would have prepared something nice for you. (Draft Script 1, Act III)

By devising and improvising around particular stories, events and characters, the spoken word was transformed from being the story of a character into a multi-layered text of many characters, some changing from historical stereotypes to contemporary representations. The first draft cited above presents Dr Ampah, an African male student of the 1950s, in a relationship with a Caribbean nurse. The character is a caricature based on historical stereotype of the fractious relationship between Africans and Black West Indians of that period. This unflattering image is transformed in the third draft, *Who Can Tell?....!* into a sensible professional who is thoroughly aware of his place in a global world:

Edwin: Yes, Maizie. That's what we're here for. How's your doctor friend?

Maizie: Kofi? Kofi's fine....

Chantal: Who's Kofi?

Maizie: Watch and all will be revealed....

(Hospital canteen: Maizie, Doctor Kofi Ampah and Aminat Hussein)

Maizie: And how long did they say they'd keep your husband quarantined?

Aminat: Until they see a significant improvement in his condition. But tell me, Dr. Ampah, do they quarantine malaria sufferers in Ghana?

Ampah: No. They're very strange here. I've told them a thousand times that malaria is not like the common cold. You can't

catch it just by being in the same room with Mr. Hussein.....
(Draft 3 'Who Can Tell?...! p24- 25)

The play is not only about people of African descent, its base was broadened to incorporate other migrants in a multicultural Britain in which race and culture continue to shape relations and society. Not only does the script lend itself to different contexts and interpretations, the performance aesthetic has also undergone radical shifts from naturalism to Brechtian epic in the course of three drafts:

(The actors change into Asian-style costume in front of the audience)

Couple A: Of course: the Asians from Uganda after Idi Amin kicked them out.

Couple B: Revitalising the corner shops and setting up curry houses.

Couple C: Not all of us ran shops and restaurants, you know.

Couple A: Some of us were professionals.

Couple B: And not all of us came from Uganda. We came from India, from Pakistan, from Bangladesh, from Sri Lanka.

Couple A: Muslims, Sikhs, Hindus, Buddhists.

(The Africans and the West Indians treat the Asians with suspicion)

Couple A: Although we were different, to our hosts we were all the same.

Couple B: They gave us a collective name.

Couple C: Forget caste or creed, religion or nation. We were Asians, all the same.

All: Asians, that's what they called us. Asians, that's the box we ticked.

Couple C: From a kaleidoscope of cultures into one little box. To make ourselves visible to the British eye....
(Draft 3 *Who Can Tell?...!* p11)

There were two writers involved on script development and the process of scripting went hand in hand with the interrogation of the resulting text. As a result, the process challenged the notions of the script as sacrosanct and as the product of sole authorship.

Stakeholder interests

The project attracted a range of interest groups from the community and the university, each with their own agendas which impacted on the working process and production outcome. The groups included Northampton Black History Association, the University's Office of Educational Partnership and Lifelong Learning (OEPLL), the University's Division of Performance Studies, the artists and performers, funding organisations such as the Arts Council of England, even performance venues. For example, the Office of Educational Partnership and Lifelong Learning, designed to nurture links between the university and its local and regional communities, funded the workshops in schools and community settings which generated additional information and audiences for the project. However, the types of activities and venues were subject to NBHA's approval. Further, NBHA's censorship of how the source materials were used moved the performance further away from verbatim theatre, which had been the initial aim. The Division of Performance Studies brought a different agenda again. It wanted the research premise foregrounded and a quick research outcome for the National Research Assessment Exercise.

The project was conceived on a voluntary basis in line with NBHA's initial Black history project. However, most of the collaborating artists and performers from the community demanded payment. This required sourcing funds from funding organisations with their own agendas which did not necessarily match those of the project on conception. The attempt to address the arising issues threatened to compromise the main aims of the project in unhelpful ways. Insufficient funds and market forces required adjusting the scope of the project as we negotiated a tension between the extent to which the resulting performance ultimately tackled questions of authenticity, ownership and even of power. The creative team was challenged by problems of confidentiality, data protection concerned with the NBHA's source material and the transformation of personal stories for the public stage.

Collaboration on the project generated tensions that impacted on the process and product, mainly due to differences in ideology and the inevitable binaries that arise: academic versus non-academic; mainstream versus fringe theatre; and the difficulties some collaborators had in understanding and working to both the concept and the spirit of collaboration. The project's dependence on the university-based participants to provide all the answers to resource and logistic issues began to project a power dynamic we had not bargained for within the creative team.

There were differences between Black cultural communities which were evident in the tendency by some to make Jamaica or the Caribbean or Africa representative of all Black communities without taking into account the heterogeneous nature of each one of these communities. Such stereotypical misrepresentations of the different communities tended to over-simplify issues. This materialised later in the kind of characters that were discussed, created, or abandoned during script development. This has provided us with a fascinating insight into how stakeholder interests, requirements and demands can impact on such a project, its aims, practices and artistic outcomes.

Closing reflections

There are limitations in working from only transcripts and audio recordings without the benefits of observing the physical language, mannerisms and gestures of the interviewees. Ordinarily, close and active engagements between research and performance processes have distinct advantages. However, where the material is pre-gathered and documented, close collaboration between partners in the production process can compensate but this did not always work as intended. For example, NBHA, unlike some of the interviewees, did not take up the offer of seeing work in progress, nor give feedback when invited to do so and they failed to comment on the regular reports on the project that we were compelled to give. While the project team responded to every request and restriction imposed by the NBHA, the organisation did not reciprocate. The lack of reciprocity was most evident in the exchange of information and in the absence of logistic support and creative input from NBHA. Such inconsistencies prolonged the performance-making process to noone's advantage.

The journey of the spoken word from oral interviews to the stage can be long, time-consuming and expensive. Because the stories belong to individuals and the community, we opted for a collaborative community theatre project that involved local artists and the owners of the stories at various stages. This, for us, meant that the research continued throughout the performance-making process and the performance became a research tool as well as a means of disseminating research findings. The various stories, interviews and historical documents generated a diverse range of materials. The materials were transformed into an original stage performance, *Who Can Tell?...!* through a rigorous process of workshops, script development and rehearsals.

We have enjoyed the breadth of the project and its spin-offs. A specially adapted version of the play was staged for young Black people in Grendon, Northampton, as part of a residential project designed to increase confidence and raise their achievement levels in school. In their final presentation at the end of the residential weekend the young people responded to some of the issues raised by the play by producing their own version entitled, *We Can Tell!* Some of the feedback from the different audiences reflect the sentiments expressed by these young people. Despite the artistic license taken on the journey, audiences could still identify with the stories. Despite the challenges, the project created a series of significant community moments:

> I really enjoyed your performances and the work of the company. I think that these stories of first generation immigrants as well as the unknown history of Black people in Northampton are such important ones to tell – and not only for the young people such as the boy and girl in the play ... It was great to see so many people from both town and university in the audience ... (Audience response to performance)

The writers acknowledge that the work would have been impossible without the interviewees, the NBHA and its oral history project, the University of Northampton's OEPLL, the collaborating artists, performers and numerous other participants. This article does not claim that this is all that the project was about. It was much more than an artistic attempt to deconstruct biographies and histories. The project and its process, script, performance and audience responses are neither fixed nor limited in context. The performance is in many ways the writers' response to Denzin's search in *Performance Ethnography: Critical Pedagogy and the Performance of Culture* for 'an interpretive social science that is simultaneously auto-ethnographic, vulnerable, performative, and critical ... that refuses abstractions and high theory... a way of being in the world, a way of writing, hearing, and listening' (2003:105).

In our experience, an ethnographic approach to Community Theatre can result in an authentic piece as we saw in this chapter. A community's involvement reinforces audiences' identification with the resulting performance. This must be real for individual audience members, as one of them expressed, for whom the material held more than cultural and historical relevance: 'The play was very very good and I could see my story being a part of the play, likewise many others in the audience.' Theatre-makers ought to be aware that ethnodrama performances need to draw their aesthetic language from the community of real people to whom personal experiences are as important as cultural histories. The outcome should, be directed to the task of restoring a sense of wholeness in the audience as a priority. Thus ethnodrama, like Victor Turner's (1974) social drama, is designed to satisfy both aesthetic and functional needs that resonate with reality. Such a role or function is only marginally present in many forms of aesthetic drama.

11

INVESTIGATING MASCULINITIES
IN SCHOOL
It's a play for us: ethnographic performance
as part of an educational ethnography

Richard Sallis

Back story

As an educational ethnographer with experience as a classroom
drama teacher, playwright, director and actor in the theatre
industry, I am keen to explore the potential of ethnographic
performance as a research method and as a narrative form with which
to share ethnographic data with teachers and students. Like many contemporary ethnographers I believe that it is important to find ways to
share my findings with the communities and cultures from which they
originated, in ways and forms that are most appropriate and accessible
for my participants. I find it both academically challenging and artistically stimulating to use dramatic presentation as a form with which to
share my research findings. I also want to explore what forms of additional data an ethnographic performance can generate when it is
written during an ongoing qualitative investigation.

I recently conducted an ethnographic research project pertaining to
classroom drama and its interrelationship with the expression of
multiple masculinities and boys' engagement in school. I subsequently
transformed my research data into an ethnographic performance.

When describing my work as an ethnodramatist I prefer to use the term ethnographic performance to refer to the ethnodramatic script and its performance. Ethnodramatist Michal McCall contends that researchers and dramatists who use this term often do so to connect their data-based play with the qualitative and ethnographic research on which it is based (2000:425). The project I conducted into boys and drama education was inter-linked with a critical consideration of the writing of an ethnographic performance as part of a school-based educational ethnography. Whilst I intended to write a conventional research report based on my investigation, ethnographic performance was to be the principal form through which I would report to my participants the inherent meanings I came to understand about their culture.

Setting the scene

My research project was conducted in a co-educational government-funded secondary school. Like most other secondary schools in Victoria, Australia, the students range in age from twelve (year seven) to eighteen (year twelve). The school is in a socially and culturally diverse inner-city community, with over 30 per cent of its residents born overseas. Young people of Anglo-Celtic and Western European backgrounds make up the majority of the student population. The gentrification of the inner-suburbs has had an impact on the social composition of the student population which is predominantly from a middle-class or professional-class home environment. A smaller proportion of students come from the government assisted housing communities nearby. All Year 7 and 8 students participate in Drama; thereafter Drama is an elective, with senior examination courses offered in Drama and in Theatre Studies.

Dramatis personae

(Pseudonyms are used throughout).

My student participants included 80 students aged between twelve and fourteen in four Year 7 classes and two Year 8 classes, and twenty combined Year 11 and 12 students aged between sixteen and eighteen.

The principal teacher participants were two female drama teachers. Ruth was Head of Drama, and taught the Year 11/12 participants. She had been teaching drama at the school for over ten years. We had previously collaborated on many panels and committees, and coincidentally her recent PhD study on drama teachers' stories, auto-ethnography and gender interconnected with mine. Sarah, in her mid-thirties, had taught drama at the school for nine years since her own graduation, and taught the year 7 and 8 classes I observed.

I also interviewed other members of staff including the School Principal and Colin, a pre-service student teacher in his twenties on placement from a local university, who taught some of Sarah's classes, which I observed.

The production team – a collaborative approach

When I was first designing this study, I invited Ruth and Sarah to work with me as co-collaborators. We agreed that the subject matter for the ethnographic performance would be boys' participation in drama because this was something that was of interest to us. We also agreed that the ethnographic performance either in its entirety, or selected scenes, would be performed by students in Ruth's senior drama class. It was significant that Ruth was involved in another ethnographic performance project outside school, where she was co-devising and co-presenting the material. She was *au fait* with the genre of ethnographic performance and some of the principal scholarship pertaining to it. Sarah did not possess Ruth's familiarity with the genre, so I shared with her a previous ethnodramatic script I had written and some related readings.

From the outset we decided that the audience for the first performance of the play would be the participants in the study. Ruth and Sarah also suggested that down the track they and their students could select scenes to be presented for school assemblies, staff professional development sessions, school open days and other public gatherings. Given that there might be other such performances, I decided to employ a convention of Brecht's epic theatre and write the play as a series of connected yet independent episodes. Thus, as required, the performance could consist of the entire play, individual scenes or vignettes grouped together around a particular theme.

Ethical considerations

When negotiating the methodological framework for the project, I informed Ruth and Sarah that I considered it my responsibility to represent the participants as I saw them. I was mindful that there could be personal and professional repercussions for the teachers and their students when the play was made public. In an attempt to circumvent such concerns, I established a set of principles which I negotiated with Ruth and Sarah, to help ensure that the perspectives of the participants were respected and appropriately represented in the play:

- the content would represent significant themes that emerged from the data and I would avoid incorporating uncharacteristic or sensationalist incidents – 'juicy bits' – merely for the sake of dramatic engagement

- any dialogue constructed for the ethnographic performance would be quoted verbatim from what was recorded either from observation or interview

- the participants' words and actions would not be imaginatively re-worked so that they were unrecognisable from their original context

- the ethnographic performance would endeavour to protect the anonymity of the participants as much as possible.

Early on, Sarah told me that she was reassured by these principles because she 'had not had [her] teaching scrutinised to this extent before' and that 'it was good to know that things would not be taken out of context ... or embellished just because they might make for good theatre'.

As it transpired, by the time I had finished writing my play I had found it necessary to re-negotiate some of these principles. There can be ethical and artistic dilemmas when a researcher concurrently works as a dramatist, trying to achieve both the distance of a scholar and engagement in artistic practice. For instance, when I embarked on writing the ethnographic performance, I found the ethical principle of avoiding material that was dramatically engaging but uncharacteristic was artistically limiting. Over the course of my data collection I often encountered an incident in a class or was told something by one of my participants which caught my interest as a dramatist. I was troubled as to whether or not to include some such data in the play, where it could potentially misrepresent what I had typically observed in the field. To help alleviate my ethical angst I adopted a method of crystallisation and included material only if it could be substantiated by other incidents and opinions I had recorded.

Prologue to the drama

Working as an educational ethnographer, I spent around thirty weeks becoming immersed in the culture of the school. From the outset, the staff and students knew that I was going to write an ethnographic performance based on my experiences with them. 'An ethnographic performance has to be about something', I explained to them, 'and in this case it is going to be about boys taking part in drama and how this affects and is affected by, the girls and other boys in the class'. I sat in on drama and other classes, interviewed staff and students, had informal conversations with them, read documents produced by the school, attended school functions where I observed and spoke to parents and other members of the school community and generally hung about in the setting. Some students shared with me their handwritten notes and workbook entries from the drama classes and gave me permission to add these to the data I could draw on when writing my ethnographic performance. As I became a more familiar face to them, the students took me more into their confidence and began to reveal deeper insights into their lives both in school and out.

The drama teachers frequently engaged with me in informal reflective conversations, generally prompted by something that had happened in their class that day. Sometimes Ruth or Sarah would describe a classroom incident, suggesting that it might 'make a good scene' for my play. As an ethnodramatist I found myself intrigued to find out what it was about the incident that gave it dramatic potential. However, as an ethnographer I was wary that perhaps Ruth and Sarah were becoming too preoccupied, too early, with the reportage of the research. Even so, I retained the information to reconsider it when I began to write my play, because evidently the drama teachers had considered it significant.

Some of the material for my ethnographic performance was collected in Sarah's Years 7 and 8 drama classes. I considered it my purpose to sit in, observe and record what took place in their classes rather than intervene or impose myself upon their teaching and learning programme. As I explained to Ruth and Sarah, it was not their responsibility to alter the way they functioned just to serve my research methods. Once I perceived that my presence in their classroom had become accepted, I began to use a tape recorder to record some of the conversations as students worked on their tasks in class. I found that the students tended to ignore the use of the recording device but at times students spoke directly into the recorder, providing reflective comments on their work. As ethnodramatist I decided that these interjections could potentially form part of the dialogue when I came to write my ethnographic performance.

By the time I began observing her senior drama class, Ruth had briefed her students about my project and they were curious and eager to work with me. Soon I found myself freely engaging with them in conversation while they were working, questioning them informally about their participation in class. I found myself making copious notes of the activities and recording any of the students' words or actions that gave insights into their behaviour. I also conducted one-on-one interviews with the senior students and focus group interviews with members of the junior classes. The transcripts of the interviews, along with my classroom observations and recordings, formed the basis of my ethnographic performance.

While I maintain that writing an ethnographic performance is in itself an analytical act, I still found myself engaging in more traditional forms of inductive data analysis. As an ethnographer I was looking to determine the themes within the data and concurrently as an ethnodramatist I was searching for dramatic action, characters and plotline elements. I engaged in a process of conceptualisation, employing qualitative coding and 'in vivo coding': codes derived from the actual words spoken by the participants. This helped me to determine particular passages from transcripts and field notes which could form part of my ethnodramatic script.

A script is not the only way to tell a story

Before I started to write my ethnodramatic script I transformed my data into narrative forms other than scripted scenes. I reasoned that transforming the data in this imaginative way freed me to organise my thoughts up to that point and to write meaning into what was emerging from the data. The narratives I wrote included fictionalised first and third person accounts of an incident and impressionistic and descriptive sketches of people and events. These were presented in various forms such as poems, songs, scrapbook collages and hand-drawn cartoons with accompanying captions which were similar to story-boarding. Applying a principle I would continue throughout the ethnodramatic process, when constructing each form of narrative writing, I quoted verbatim, from speech I had recorded in the field. Whilst playing with the narrative writing in this way was time-consuming, I found it most fulfilling because it enabled me further to gauge the dramatic potential of the data. The narrative pieces which were the most dramatically engaging and meaningful were re-worked into dialogue and action for my performance.

Limitations of the data

In a standard qualitative research report an argument is developed and text derived from verbatim accounts may be included to help validate the contentions. I have found that when writing an ethnographic performance the words of the participants need to serve both of these purposes: the dialogue and the actions of the characters need to encapsulate the research findings as well as provide the evidential support for the contentions. While this act of data and dialogue retrieval was often finicky, it was more artistically satisfying than writing a conventional research report. The content of my script was determined by the volume of data I had available and its relevance to the overall concepts of my research enquiry. While this may be akin to any qualitative researcher writing up their findings, I found it to be particularly limiting and frustrating because of the pact I had made with my participants that the content of my ethnographic performance would be constructed entirely from conversations and incidents which occurred in the field and from the interviews I had conducted. I was reluctant to alter this stance because my participants had informed me how reassuring this was for them.

I decided to cut myself some artistic slack. I negotiated with Ruth and Sarah that I would create a fictional framework for the ethnographic performance. As I explained to them, the drama classrooms depicted in the play would be 'made up of bits' of several classes I had observed, 'cut-and-pasted together'. I would also create composite characters made up from individuals I had observed who had exhibited similar traits.

Sharing the emerging text – entering into the dialogic

Sharing the emerging script of my ethnographic performance with my participants was a vital stage in the ethnodramatic process. It provided further verification of what I had observed, recorded and transcribed; it served a dramaturgical function because my participants assisted me to determine the content and form of my ethnographic performance; it generated additional data associated with the foci of my research project. The first time I shared the emerging script with my student participants I placed them in focus groups and showed them excerpts that were based on their particular class. They were entitled to feel comfortable that I was not revealing material about them to others before they had a chance to comment on it. With my student participants I established an informal rehearsal, which we called a 'mini performance', where they read the script aloud, sometimes adding body gestures, facial expressions and impromptu scenic blocking. During these sessions we discussed the meanings that emanated from the script and its performance. I encouraged them to suggest additions or deletions. This reciprocity generated new ethnographic data, including how the students participated in the drama classes and additional background information on the scenes I had written.

Anonymity is an issue for any ethnographer working in a small community. This may be exacerbated when writing an ethnographic performance because findings are shared in a public way, including with the participants. The Year 8 focus groups, who were the first to read the scenes I had drafted, were curious to find out 'who is who', which I understood to mean: which characters represented which students in their class. I reassured them that to protect their identity I had created composite characters. But it was soon apparent that the students were not pleased with this decision. Fitz told me bluntly: 'Well you might have tried to disguise who we are, but it is pretty obvious anyway. Like the character of Orson. He has bits of Oscar and bits of Trevor in him. It's so obvious'.

Others agreed. Angelica and Lara could both see themselves in the character of Bridget. Angelica told me, 'I remember that class so well. I said some of those things and Lara said some of them. I reckon other people in our class will remember too, so why try to hide it? What's the point?'

I explained to her: 'Given that ethnographic performances are based on real people and what they say and do, if it is too obvious to other people who the characters are based on, the real person might get teased or get into trouble because of what the character does or says in the play'.

I then spoke with Oscar and Trevor, who as Fitz had rightly ascertained, jointly contributed to the character of Orson. I was particularly interested to hear their views given that in the play Orson is often reprimanded by the drama teacher. Interestingly, both students appeared unconcerned that others might identify them in my script. Oscar elucidated, 'look it's not as if we didn't do the things you've put in [the script]. If you'd put something in there that wasn't true that would be different ... But if we did it, then we did it, and that's okay'.

Karen, another Year 8 student, provided further insight: 'I think if you want to use something I did in class in the script then that's fine, but I don't like the idea of having it changed, by you making up a person who wasn't really there'.

Students in other classes who were asked about this issue had a similar view. Daisy, a Year 11 drama student, informed me that 'we have such a lot of different personality types in our class but our class is not very big and so their views are well known. They come across in what the characters say'.

Given that most students wanted me to abandon the practice of creating composite characters, I took the question of anonymity further and asked them whether I should also abandon using pseudonyms as well. The consensus was that it was necessary to give them a pseudonym to conceal their identity from others outside their class. Violet, a year 8 student, encapsulated the opinion of many when she told me 'it's more important that other people, like teachers, don't know who we are. People in our class might recognise us, but that's okay because they were there anyway'.

This feedback from the students left me wondering whether I might abandon another of the ethical principles I had established for this project. I shared my concerns with the drama staff. Together we decided that the characters' names would remain pseudonyms and in response to the student feedback each of the main student characters would be based on a particular student in the drama classes. However, I decided that I would still create some composite characters as well. These 'Every-student' characters would comment on the action on stage, share additional insights about the culture and encapsulate the viewpoints of many of the students I had observed and interviewed.

Even though drama is a popular subject at this school, I was unprepared for the level of interest and insight the student participants showed in my ethnodramatic processes. For instance, the junior students were keen to discuss why I had chosen certain incidents to include in the play rather than others. Some reminded me of things they had said and done that they thought were worthy of inclusion. While I welcomed their feedback, I explained that the content of the play was representative of many similar incidents I had observed and that it was impossible to include everything. But I did add some material to the play based on student feedback, especially when it enhanced the understanding of the events I had already included.

One result of dispensing with the composite protagonist characters was that in later drafts of the play many of the student participants could easily recognise themselves or their classmates. In what Ruth, Sarah and I referred to as the Reality-TV syndrome students at all levels were fixated on how the characters based on them would appear to the audience and how an actor portraying them in the play might make judgements about the real person behind the character. When reading the revised draft of the scenes in which they were featured, there were squeals of delight and howls of feigned horror as students recognised characters based on themselves or their peers. With this recognition came a barrage of questions and comments such as 'Who will play me?', 'In the script I giggle a lot. Do you think they [the actors] will think I giggle all the time?' 'Do you think I come across as a nice person?' 'God, I sound like such a dumb-arse in that scene'.

All ethnographers have to make decisions about what to share about their participants in their research reports, but my experience with a Year 7 boy called Murphy reminded me what is potentially at stake for informants in a project where the findings will be shared in a play. Having read a scene in which he could recognise himself, Murphy asked me 'is that how you see me, as a figure of fun?' As this was not my intention I asked him, 'why do you think I was making fun of you?' His reply: 'Because each time I open my mouth I sound like a nerd'. I explained to Murphy that 'I put that dialogue in the play because I thought what you had to say was really interesting and very mature. I am sorry if you think it looks as if I was making fun of you'. After this initial exchange I was troubled by Murphy's reaction because I agreed with the valid point he was making; as the ethnodramatist I had selectively chosen what to include about Murphy in my play and he was reacting to those choices. I wondered how many other students were concerned, like Murphy, about the choices that I had made on their behalf. I could not let this rest. I went back to Murphy and suggested we go over my original data together to help 'balance up his character'. He welcomed this initiative. Not only did I learn more about Murphy but I benefitted from his take on the ethnographic data I had previously recorded about his class. From my perspective of the ethnodramatist, this incident strongly affirmed the immense value of such dialogic exchanges with participants during the writing of an ethnographic performance. Concomitantly, as an ethnographer I found that sharing the emerging script with participants can generate rich detail, opinions and perspectives that may otherwise remain hidden.

I also shared the emerging script with the drama teachers and we discussed how they were being represented. Ruth, Sarah and Colin were comfortable with me constructing scenes depicting them teaching their classes. I gave them pseudonyms to disguise their identity from others outside their school. However, we reasoned that we had to accept that those within their school would easily be able to identify them by their teaching style, the classes they taught and other identifiable characteristics. In our early discussions all three teachers preferred me not to include in the play, discussions we had had about easily identifiable students and incidents. For Sarah, 'some of the talks we ... have had have been as drama colleagues, and perhaps they are best left as that, rather than ending up [in the] play'.

Similarly, Colin observed, 'Look, I'm sure the kids know we talk about them out of class and that sort of thing, but they don't expect to be in on those conversations. I think it is important, even with what you're doing, that we keep some professional distance.'

With reference to her Year 12 Drama class, Ruth quipped, 'I am sure they know what I think of them anyway'. However she was concerned that if the ethnographic performance included discussions she had had with me about particular students, this could adversely affect how they might respond 'once they have read what I said about them'.

A matter of style and form

As with other forms of qualitative research reportage, the stylistic choices made when writing an ethnographic performance are important, especially when the participants have a particular interest and expertise in drama and theatre. In Victoria, a style generically well-known to local drama teachers as 'non-naturalism' dominates the Years 11 and 12 Drama courses. I decided to incorporate conventions of non-naturalism into my ethnographic performance because this was an aesthetic form that the teachers and students were used to working within. As I had found in a previous school-based research study, a convention of non-naturalism that lends itself to the presentation of an ethnographic performance is the breaking of the fourth wall between the actors and audience. In my previous project the non-naturalistic actor-audience relationship facilitated a dialogue between them during the ethnographic performance and fostered a productive discussion afterwards.

When I observed Ruth working with her year 11 and 12 VCE Drama students I took note of the various non-naturalistic techniques they used. As well as direct address to the audience, these included soliloquies and asides, disjointed time-sequences, transformation of time, place and object, movement and mime sequences and techniques of Poor Theatre (Grotowski, 1968). One non-naturalistic technique Ruth taught her students was for the dialogue to capture the essence of meaning, rather than reproduce natural speech. This had a profound effect on the later drafts of my play. Whilst still quoting verbatim from my data, I attempted to adopt a pared-back approach to dialogue, in keeping with this technique. I also conducted my own research beyond Ruth's drama classroom to find out the range of techniques that senior students in schools in Victoria use when working on non-naturalistic performances. This led me to incorporate conventions based on Boal's 'cop in the head' (1992:192) and 'thought tracking', where the thoughts of a character are conveyed to the audience by another actor. I found these techniques useful in providing a reflective voice for the participants and this added a deeper subtext to the dramatic action. I noticed that Ruth's senior students incorporated multimedia into their performances in their class work. In an attempt to work within the same aesthetic as the students, I decided to include the use of theatre technologies in the script of my ethnographic performance. For instance, throughout the play a data show is screened to accompany the on-stage action. It includes pre-recorded footage, live camera work and streaming of Internet sites, all of which depict relevant resource material about the context and content of the play.

The inclusion of a narrator is a common convention in ethnographic performances. The narrator, who is sometimes the voice of the ethnodramatist, unpacks the content of the piece for the audience. Early in the writing process Sarah and I discussed whether or not I should have a narrator in the play. We speculated that this character could perhaps perform an exegesis function. But Sarah thought that this might shift the focus away from the student and teacher characters so I decided not to pursue it.

Negotiating the performance

Apart from my interest in boys and how they operate in drama, the principal focus of my research was to examine the usefulness of an ethnographic performance written as part of an educational ethnography from the perspective of the participants and the researcher. As the researcher I was keen to let my subjects help steer the writing and presentation of the play. From early in the project I stressed to Ruth and Sarah that I did not expect the drama department to mount a performance of my play just to fulfil my research agenda. I explained that 'because I am keen to see how useful it is to you [the drama staff] that I write an ethnographic performance as part of this project, I would like you to decide what happens to it, once it's written'. But it was evident from early in the fieldwork that Ruth and Sarah both envisaged that the play would be performed. As it transpired a number of factors were to influence when the play was performed, by whom and the form that it was to take.

In this study I wanted to engage in a prolonged period where I shared the various drafts of the script with my participants so they could have greater ownership of it, and I would learn more about them and their culture through our reflective conversations. During the months of the drafting process there were many 'mini-performances' when students workshopped the scripted material as I produced it. Even though the students were becoming familiar with my ethnographic performance through the drafting process, Ruth, Sarah and I felt that there needed to be a formal presentation of the full play script. However, because the year 12 students were about to leave school and had been such an integral part of the process, we decided to mount a Reader's Theatre performance, presented by members of the senior drama class and the drama teachers; the student participants would be its principal audience.

Although the senior Drama students had seen excerpts of the play before, they had not experienced it in its entirety until the Reader's Theatre performance. The performance had an air of excitement, joviality and a high level of discussion. From an ethnographer's standpoint, it was satisfying to see how the students and staff expressed their opinions freely, especially about boys participating in drama, which was the main theme of the play. Even though they were engaged in a staged reading of the play, the staff and student performers embodied the characters and used a range of acting and expressive skills. It struck me as significant that when portraying the schoolboy characters both male and female performers reproduced aspects of male performance through vocal expression, gesture and bodily physicalisation. As they did so, others provided feedback on their portrayal or side-coached them. For instance; 'His voice is deeper than that'; 'Yes, that's just how Year 7s walk'; 'I remember that boys sat around like that when I was in year eight'; 'Boys can sound so domineering in class, can't they?' It was not until the full play was presented in this way that I fully appreciated that, like the enactment of the 'mini performances', the presentation of an ethnographic performance to an audience by a group of actors can generate data that a passive reading of the script cannot. The performances during the drafting process and this culminating one gave my participants the opportunity to embody the characters and this connected them more deeply to the incidents depicted in the text.

Although the Reader's Theatre performance was a success, I was left with a feeling of disappointment afterwards, wondering what the effect might have been had we staged a fully rehearsed version of the play. Ruth and Sarah did not share my misgivings, however. They maintained that because the play was about *them* and *their* Drama programme, it was up to the participants to decide how and for whom it was staged.

Sarah: and	*[This] has been enough for us... If the kids had acted it out in a conventional way, you would have had an extra audience I guess. But then it becomes more about the production of it you may get away from the opportunity of the people in it to comment on it.*
Ruth:	*I think there was something quite special giving us the opportunity to play ourselves or each other; and making that decision.*
Sarah:	*Yes, I guess it's a play for us, our school... but that it was so about our particular culture, meant that it was up to us what to do with it – what suited us and our needs.*

(Excerpt from the ethnographic performance, *It's A Play for Us*)

The usefulness of ethnographic performance in a school setting

After my ethnographic performance was presented I met up with Ruth and Sarah over the following months because I wanted to understand better how useful the play had been for them. I also contacted some of the student participants to find out how they had been affected by it. Ruth and Sarah informed me that my presence in their school as both ethnographer and ethnodramatist had prompted them to undergo a process of reflective practice. According to Ruth, the process made her 'think a lot more about our drama boys, the shy ones ... the nerds and the misfits'.

For Sarah, my ethnographic performance 'had highlighted the gender dynamics' in her classes and 'provided [her] with new insights about how the [male and female] students work together'. Sarah noted that she had 'benefitted from the effects' of the project. In regard to the teaching of boys in drama my ethnographic performance had 'showed [her] things about [her] teaching which were picked up on' and which she had 'decided to concentrate on' when teaching her classes in the future.

I asked the drama staff whether they would have got as much out of a conventional ethnographic research report. Ruth said that for her an ethnodramatic script 'was a very accessible way of showing what happens in the [drama] classes' at her school and she could 'see the potential' of the ways in which it, 'could be used to show other staff and parents what goes on in drama and how much the kids get out of it, especially the boys'.

The school Principal informed me that he considered the form of reportage to 'be something different; something that [he could see] parents enjoying and benefitting from'. He told me that 'we have a lot of researchers come to our school and we don't always get to find out immediately, sometimes not at all, what their findings were ... but your play is potentially a good way for us as a staff to learn from what you've found out'.

For Sarah, 'one of the delights' of the project was that 'it [was] about the writing of a play ... something that [she] could respond to both intellectually and aesthetically'.

This notion was echoed by Bob, one of the senior drama students. On the day he performed the play he told me:

> What's good about this [the ethnographic performance] is that it is play and we are drama students. It kind of – I know this sounds clichéd – but it kind of 'speaks our language'... and I mean what better way to tell drama students things about drama than with a play?

References

Ackroyd, J and Pilkington, A (2008) *Artistry Versus Purpose in the Design of Vocational Programmes: drama and anti-racism in police training*. The Sixth International Conference on new directions in the Humanities. Faith University. Istanbul, Turkey

Alexander, B (2005) Performance Ethnography: the re-enacting and inciting of culture. In N K Denzin and Y S Lincoln (eds) *The Sage Handbook of Qualitative Research*. London: Sage Publications

Anderson, M (2007) Making Theatre from Data: lessons for performative ethnography from verbatim theatre. NJ (*Journal of Drama Australia*) 31/1 p79-91

Arnold, R (2005) *Empathic Intelligence: teaching, learning, relating*. Sydney: University of New South Wales Press

Aronson, L (2000) *Scriptwriting Updated; new and conventional ways of writing for the screen*. Australian Film, Radio and Television School. Sydney: Allen and Unwin

Bacon, J (2006) The Feeling of the Experience: a methodology for performance ethnography. In J Ackroyd (ed) *Research Methodologies for Drama Education*. Stoke on Trent: Trentham Books

Bagley, C and Cancienne, M B (2001). Educational Research and Intertextual Forms of (Re)presentation: the case for dancing the Data. In *Dancing the data*. New York: Peter Lang.

Bakhtin, M (1981) *The Dialogic Imagination: four essays*. Edited by Michael Holquist, translated by Caryl Emerson and Michael Holquist. Austin: University of Texas Press.

Barone, T (2002) From Genre Blurring to Audience Blending: reflections on the field emanating from an ethnodrama. *Anthropology and Education Quarterly* 33 (2) pp255-267

Behar, R (2008) Anthropology: ethnography and the book that was lost. In J G Knowles and A L Cole (eds) *Handbook of the Arts in Qualitative Research: perspectives, methodologies, examples, and issues*. California: Sage Publications

Beja, M (1979) *Film and Literature – an introduction*. London: Longman

Boal, A (1992) *Games for Actors and Non-actors*. London: Routledge

Bowles, K (2006) Representation. In S Cunningham and G Turner (eds) *The Media and Communications in Australia, 2nd edition*. Crows Nest: Allen and Unwin

Brecht, B (1964) The Street Scene. In: Willett, J (ed. and trans.) *Brecht on Theatre: the development of an aesthetic.* London: Methuen.

Brown, D (1998) *Keep Everything You Love.* Theatre in Education. Brisbane: Brisbane Festival

Brown, P and the Workers' Cultural Action Committee (1993) *Aftershocks.* Strawberry Hills: Currency Press

Bundy, P (2006) Reflective Practice and the Playwright/Scholar. NJ (*Drama Australia Journal*) 30 (2) pp51-59

Butler, J (1990) *Gender Trouble: feminism and the subversion of identity.* New York: Routledge

Carlson, M (1996) *Performance: a critical introduction,* London: Routledge

Cheeseman, P (2005) On Documentary Theatre. In R Soans *Talking to Terrorists.* London: Oberon

Clandinin, J and Connelly, M (2000) *Narrative Inquiry, Experience and Story in Qualitative Research.* San Francisco: Jossey-Bass

Connell, R W (2002) *Gender.* Malden, Cambridge: Polity Press in association with Blackwell Publishers

Conquergood, D (1991) Rethinking Ethnography: towards a critical cultural politics. In *Communication Monographs*, 59 pp179-104

Conquergood, D (2003) Performing as a Moral Act: ethical dimensions of the ethnography of performance. In N K Denzin and Y S Lincoln (eds.) *Turning Points in Qualitative Research, Tying Knots in a Handkerchief.* Walnut Creek, CA: AltaMira Press.

Courtney, R (1990) *Drama and Intelligence: a cognitive theory.* Montreal: McGill-Queens University Press

Cozart, S, Gordon, J, Gunzenhauser, M, Mckinney, M and Petterson, J (2003). Disrupting Dialogue: envisioning performance ethnography for research and evaluation. *Educational Foundations* 17 (2) pp53-79

Davies, B, Browne, J, Gannon, S, Honan, E, and Somerville, M (2005) Embodied Women at Work in Neoliberal Times and Places. *Gender, Work and Organisation* 12 (4) pp343-362

Denzin, N (1997) *Interpretive Ethnography: ethnographic practices for the 21st century.* Thousand Oaks, Cal: Sage

Denzin, N (2003) *Performance Ethnography: critical pedagogy and the performance of culture.* London: Sage Publications

Denzin, N. (2004). Lecture: Arizona State University, Tempe. Reported in J. Saldaña (ed) (2006) *Ethnodrama: an anthology of reality theatre.* Walnut Creek: Altamira

Denzin, N and Lincoln, Y (2006) Foreword. In J. Saldaña (ed) *Ethnodrama: an anthology of reality theatre.* Walnut Creek: Altamira

DfES (2002) *Every Child Matters.* London: Department for Education and Skills

DfES/DH (2003) *Together From the Start.* London: Department for Education and Skills/Department of Health

REFERENCES

Donmoyer R and Yennie-Donmoyer J (1995) Data as Drama: reflections on the use of reader's theatre as a mode of qualitative data display. *Qualitative Inquiry* 1 (4) pp402-420

Donmoyer, R, and Yennie-Donmoyer J (1998) Reader's Theatre in Educational Research – give me a for instance: a commentary on Womentalkin. *International Journal of Qualitative Studies in Education* 11 (3) p397-407.

Donmoyer, R. and Yennie-Donmoyer, J (2008) Reader's Theater as a Data Display Strategy. In J G Knowles and A L Cole (eds.) *Handbook of the Arts in Qualitative Research: perspectives*, methodologies, examples and issues. Thousand Oaks, CA: Sage Publications.

Eagleton, T (1991) *Ideology: an introduction.* London: Verso Press

Easthope, A and McGowan, K (eds.) (1992) *A Critical and Cultural Theory Reader,* London: Oxford University Press.

Egan, K (1988) *Imagination and Education.* New York: Teachers' College Press

Favorini, A (2003) History, Collective Memory and Aeschylus's Persians. *Theatre Journal,* Vol 55(1), pp99-111

Gaul, K (2005) *Interview* conducted by M Anderson and L Wilkinson. Sydney University, 29 June 2008

Giddings, R, Selby, K and Wensley, C (1990) *Screening the Novel.* Macmillan 'Insights'

Gillham, G (1974) The Condercum Project. Unpublished Monograph: Durham University, UK

Goldman, D (2007) Dwight in the Deep Pine Woods, *Cultural Studies* 21 (6) pp832-836

Goldstein, T (2002) Performed Ethnography for Representing Other People's Children in Critical Educational Research. *The Applied Theatre Researcher/IDEA Journal 3*

Goodall, J (1986) *The Chimpanzees of Gombe: patterns of behaviour.* Cambridge, Mass: Harvard University Press

Gray, R, Sinding, C, Ivonoffski, V, Fitch M, Hampson, A and Greenberg, M (2000) The Use of Research-based Theatre in a Project Related to Metastatic Breast Cancer. *Health Expectations* 3 pp137-144

Grotowski, J (1968) *Towards a Poor Theatre.* New York: Simon and Shuster

Hall, S, Critcher, C, Clarke, J and Roberts, B (1978) *Policing The Crisis – mugging, the state and law and order.* London: MacMillan

Henry, M (2000) Drama's Ways of Learning. *Research in Drama Education* 5 (1) pp45-63

Hobsbaum, P (1970) The Appreciation of Minor Art. In: *A Theory of Communication*, London: Macmillan

Holderness, G (ed) (1992) *The Politics of Theatre and Drama.* London: Macmillan

Horin, R (2004) Through the Wire. Unpublished play script

Horin, R (2005) *Interview* conducted by M Anderson and Li Wilkinson. Rose Bay, NSW. June 9, 2008

Jones, J L (2002) Performance Ethnography: the role of embodiment in cultural authenticity. In *Theatre Topics*, Vol 12 No 1 pp1-14

Kaufman, M and the Tectonic Theater Project (2001) *The Laramie Project.* New York: Vintage Books

Lather, P (2000) 'How Research can be Made to Mean: feminist ethnography at the limits of representation' Keynote address at International Drama in Education Research Institute, Ohio State University

Lorenz, K (1964) *King Solomon's Ring: new light on animal ways.* London: Methuen

Luttrell, W (2000) Good Enough Methods for Ethnographic Research. *Harvard Educational Review* 70 (4) pp499-524

MacIntyre, A (1985) *After Virtue: a study in moral theory.* London: Duckworth

Macrae N and Pardue K (2007) Use of Reader's Theatre to Enhance Interdisciplinary Geriatric Education. *Educational Gerontology* 33 (6) pp529-536

McCall, M (2000) Performance Ethnography, a Brief History and Some Advice. In N K Denzin and Y S Lincoln (eds) *Handbook of Qualitative Research,* Second Edition. Thousand Oaks: Sage Publications

McInerney, P (2000) *Interim Report of the Special Commission of Inquiry into the Glenbrook Rail Accident.* Sydney: Crown Solicitor's Department

Madison, D (2005) *Critical Ethnography.* Thousand Oaks, Cal: Sage

Mienczakowski, J (1994) Reading and Writing Research. NJ: *Journal of Drama Australia* 18 (2) pp45-54

Mienczakowski, J (1994) Theatrical and Theoretical Experimentation in Ethnography and Dramatic Form. In: *Drama: One Forum Many Voices* (2) pp16-23

Mienczakowski, J (1994) The Application of Critical Ethno Drama to Health Settings. In *Mask*, Vol. 16. No. 4. Melbourne: Victorian Association for Drama In Education

Mienczakowski, J and Morgan, S (1994) *Synching Out Loud: a journey into illness: a research report.* Brisbane: Griffith University

Mienczakowski, J (1997) Theatre of Change. *Research in Drama Education* 2 (2) pp159-172

Mienczakowski, J. (1999). Emerging Forms: comments upon Johnny Saldaña's 'Ethical Issues in an Ethnographic Text: the 'dramatic impact of juicy stuff'. *Research in Drama Education.* 4 (1) pp97-100

Mienczakowski, J (2001) Ethnodrama: performed research – limitations and potential. In P Atkinson (ed) *Handbook of Ethnography.* Thousand Oaks Cal: Sage

Mienczakowski, J. (2001). Ethnodrama: constructing participatory, experiential and compelling action research through performance. In *Handbook of Action Research, Participative Inquiry and Practice* P. Reason and H. Bradbury (eds.). London: Sage Publications

Mienczakowski, J, Smith, L and Morgan, S (2002) *Seeing Words – Hearing Feelings.* In C Bagley and M B Cancienne (eds) Dancing the data. New York: Peter Lang

Mienczakowski, J (2003) The Theater of Ethnography: the reconstruction of ethnography into theater with emancipatory potential. In N K Denzin and Y S Lincoln (eds)

Turning Points in Qualitative Research: tying knots in a handkerchief. Walnut Creek: Altamira Press

Mienczakowski, J and Moore, T (2008) Performing Data with Notions of Responsibility. In J G Knowles and A L Cole (Eds) *Handbook of the Arts in Qualitative Inquiry: perspectives, methodologies, examples and issues.* Thousand Oaks CA: Sage Publications.

Nicholson, H (1999) Research as Confession. *Research in Drama Education* 4 (1) pp100-104

Nicholson, H (2003) The Performance of Memory: drama, reminiscence and autobiography. NJ: *Journal of Drama Australia* 27 (2) pp71-92

Northampton Black History Project (2003) *Newsletter,* Vol. 1, Issue 1

Northampton Black History Project (2004) *The Black History Project Oral Archive: Summaries of the Oral History Interview,* Vol. 1

O'Toole, J (2003) *Through a Glass, Darkly – re-evaluating ethnodrama.* Paper presented at 4th International Drama in Education Institute, Northampton, July.

O'Toole, J (2006) *Doing Drama Research: stepping into enquiry in drama, theatre and education.* Brisbane: Drama Australia.

Paget, D (1987) Verbatim Theatre: oral history and documentary techniques. *New Theatre Quarterly* 3 (12) pp317-336

Pardue, K (2004) Introducing Readers Theater! a strategy to foster aesthetic knowing in nursing. *Nurse Educator* 29 (2) pp58-62

Pelias, R (2008) Performative Inquiry: embodiment and its challenges. In J G Knowles and A L Cole (eds) *Handbook of the Arts in Qualitative Research: perspectives, methodologies, examples, and issues.* California: Sage Publications

Probyn, E (2003) The Spatial Imperative of Subjectivity. In K Anderson, M Domosh, S Pile and N Thrift (eds) *Handbook of Cultural Geography.* London: Sage Publications

Richardson, L (1990) *Writing Strategies: reaching diverse audiences.* London: Sage

Richardson, L (2000) Writing: a method of inquiry. In N K Denzin and Y S Lincoln (eds) *Handbook of Qualitative Research,* second edition. California: Sage Publications

Robinson J and Young J (2007) *Encounters: a reader's theatre script exploring experiences of care co-ordination for children with complex needs.* Norwich: UEA

Rowe, N (2007) *Playing the Other: dramatizing personal narratives in playback theatre,* London: Jessica Kingsley Publishers

Saldaña, J (1998) Ethical issues in an Ethnographic Performance Text: the 'dramatic impact of 'juicy stuff'. In *Research in Drama Education,* 3 (2) pp181-196

Saldaña, J (2003) Dramatizing Data: a primer. *Qualitative Inquiry* 9 (2) pp218-236

Saldaña, J (2005) *Ethnodrama: an anthology of reality theatre.* Walnut Creek. CA: Altamira

Saldaña, J (2008) Ethnodrama and Ethnotheatre. In J G Knowles and A L Cole (Eds.) *Handbook of the Arts in Qualitative Research: perspectives, methodologies, examples and issues.* Thousand Oaks, CA: Sage Publications

Sallis, R (2008) It's a Play for Us: an ethnographic performance about boys' participation in classroom drama. Unpublished manuscript

Sallis, R (2004) Masculinities and Drama. Unpublished M.Ed thesis, The University of Melbourne

Sallis, R (2009) Investigating Boys and Masculinities in Mixed School Drama Classes. Unpublished PhD thesis, The University of Melbourne.

Schechner, R (1985) *Between Theatre and Anthropology.* Philadelphia, PA: University of Pennsylvania Press

Sinyard, N (1986) *Filming Literature.* London: Croom Helm

Smith, A (1993) *Fires in the Mirror: Crown Heights Brooklyn and other identities.* New York: Anchor Books

Smith, C and Gallo, A (2007) Applications of Performance Ethnography in Nursing. *Qualitative Health Research* 17 pp521-528

Somers, J (1996) Approaches to Drama Research. In *Research in Drama Education,* 1 (2) pp165-173

Stone-Mediatore, S (2003) *Reading across Borders: storytelling and postcolonial struggles.* Basingstoke: Palgrave Macmillan

Turner, V (1974) *Drama, Fields and Metaphors: symbolic action in human society,* Ithaca: Cornell University Press

Turner, V (1982) *From Ritual to Theatre: the human seriousness of play.* New York: Performing Arts Journal Publications

Turner, V and Bruner, E (eds) (1986) *The Anthropology of Experience.* Urbana, IL: University of Illinois Press

Turner, V (1986) *The Anthropology of Performance.* New York: Performing Arts Journal Publications

Turner, V (1991) Dramatic Ritual/Ritual Drama: performative and reflective anthropology. In Bonnie Marranca and Gautam Dasgupta, (eds) (1991) *Interculturalism and Performance. Writings from PAJ.* New York: PAJ publications

Wagner, G (1975) *The Novel and the Cinema.* Rutherford, N.J.: Fairleigh Dickinson University Press

Weems, M E (2002) *Public Education and the Imagination-intellect: I speak from the wound in my mouth.* New York: Peter Lang

Wilkinson, L (2008) Creating Verbatim Theatre – exploring the gap between Public Inquiry and private pain. Unpublished Masters Thesis, University of Sydney

Wilkinson, L (2009) A Day in December. Unpublished playscript

Wright, D (2004) *I Am My Own Wife.* New York: Faber and Faber

Young, J and Robinson, J (2005) An Evaluation of the Norfolk Care Co-ordination Initiatives: final report. Norwich: UEA

Website

http://www.livingarchive.org.uk (Retrieved 24 June 2009)

Index